COMBAT AIRCRAFT

145 MACCHI C.202/C.205V UNITS IN COMBAT

SERIES EDITOR TONY HOLMES

145

COMBAT AIRCRAFT

Marco Mattioli

MACCHI C.202/C.205V UNITS IN COMBAT

OSPREY
PUBLISHING

OSPREY PUBLISHING

Bloomsbury Publishing Plc

Kemp House, Chawley Park, Cumnor Hill, Oxford, OX2 9PH, UK

29 Earlsfort Terrace, Dublin 2, Ireland

1385 Broadway, 5th Floor, New York, NY 10018, USA

E-mail; info@ospreypublishing.com

www.ospreypublishing.com

OSPREY is a trademark of Osprey Publishing Ltd

First published in Great Britain in 2022

A catalogue record for this book is available from the British Library.

ISBN: PB 9781472850683; eBook 9781472850690; ePDF 9781472850706;
XML 9781472850676

22 23 24 25 26 10 9 8 7 6 5 4 3 2 1

Edited by Tony Holmes
Cover Artwork by Gareth Hector
Aircraft Profiles by Richard Caruana
Index by Zoe Ross
Typeset by PDQ Digital Media Solutions, UK
Printed and bound in India by Replika Press Private Ltd

Osprey Publishing supports the Woodland Trust, the UK's leading woodland
conservation charity.

To find out more about our authors and books visit **www.ospreypublishing.com**.
Here you will find extracts, author interviews, details of forthcoming events and
the option to sign up for our newsletter.

Dedication

To 4° *Stormo* ace Generale Emanuele Annoni, former wartime *Folgore* pilot
Comandante Felice Figus, and to all aviators who flew both the C.202 and the
C.205V in World War 2. I would also like to dedicate this volume to my nephew
Paolo, who is a genuine aeroplane enthusiast, and to my father Fabrizio, who
taught me to love history.

Front Cover

On 6 July 1942, C.202s from 20° *Gruppo*
sortied from Sicily to provide indirect escort
for three Z.1007bis of 9° *Stormo* (which had
14 Re.2001s from 2° *Gruppo* as close
escort) heading for Luqa/Mqabba airfield on
Malta. Amongst the fighters involved were
eight 151ª *Squadriglia* C.202s led by
Capitano Furio Niclot Doglio with Maresciallo
Ennio Tarantola, being one of his wingmen.

When 11 Spitfire VCs from No 249 Sqn
– led by Flt Lt Norman Lee – scrambled to
intercept the approaching formation, Niclot
Doglio's Macchis immediately engaged
them. Future ranking Malta Spitfire ace Sgt
George Beurling quickly claimed a 'Macchi'
shot down. His victim was actually a
Re.2001, whose pilot bailed out. Beurling
then chased after the C.202 flown by five-
victory ace Sergente Maggiore Francesco
Pecchiari of 352ª *Squadriglia*, pursuing him
from 20,000 ft down to 5000 ft, where the
Folgore 'blew up' and the pilot was killed.

The remaining C.202 pilots then
counterattacked, with Niclot Doglio claiming
a Spitfire shot down. Its demise was
witnessed by Tarantola, who saw the 'British'
fighter crash north of Valetta. He had actually
seen the demise of the Re.2001 claimed by
Beurling. Another Spitfire was claimed by
Tenente Michele Gallo near St Paul's Bay. In
reality, no Spitfires had been lost, although
Plt Off A S Yates' fighter had been so badly
damaged he was forced to crash-land and
Sgt Beurling's fighter was found to be
severely holed upon his return to base (*Cover
artwork by Gareth Hector*)

Previous Pages

Brand new C.202 *Serie VII* MM9044 was
photographed at Lonate Pozzolo airfield
immediately prior to it being delivered to the
Regia Aeronautica. A total of 100 *Serie VII
Folgores* were built by Macchi between April
and July 1942 (*Philip Jarrett Collection*)

Acknowledgements

The author would like to thank all those who
have supported him in the preparation of this
book, specifically Luogotenente Maurizio Di
Terlizzi of the Customs Guard, Boris Ciglic,
Federico Figus, Milan Micevski, Dr David
Nicolle, Claudio Panebianco, Dragan Savic,
Colonnello Fabrizio Giardini (Head of the
Italian Army General Staff Historical Office)
and Colonnello Edoardo Grassia (Head of the
Italian Air Force Historical Archive). Thank you
also to the following personnel from the
Italian Air Force Photographic Service – Head
Tenente Colonnello Gianluca Pasqualini,
Primi Luogotenenti Luca Grande and Lorenzo
Fusco and Primi Marescialli Renato Bottiglia
and Antonio Stellato. Finally, the editor would
like to thank Giorgio Apostolo, Philip Jarrett,
Giovanni Massimello and Andrew Thomas for
the provision of photographs for this book.

CONTENTS

CHAPTER ONE

ULTIMATE MACCHI FIGHTERS

Following a series of flawed pre-war evaluations that convinced the leadership of the *Regia Aeronautica* to opt for radial engines rather than inline powerplants due to the former being more reliable and less complicated, Italy entered World War 2 in June 1940 with its fighter units equipped with obsolescent Macchi C.200 and Fiat G.50 monoplanes and Fiat CR.32 and CR.42 biplanes.

In the early actions that ensued, on the Italian border with France, in the Balkans and in Africa, it soon became evident that despite the skill of Italian fighter pilots, their underpowered and under-armed aircraft were not a match for modern Allied fighters powered by reliable inline engines that on average produced around 1000 hp. By contrast, the Fiat radials fitted in C.200s, G.50s and CR.42s could barely muster 870 hp. To make matters worse, French and British fighters were usually armed with up to eight machine guns (the Dewoitine D.520, Morane-Saulnier MS.406 and Bloch MB.150 series fighters even had 20 mm cannon). Italian fighters started the war with just two 7.7 mm machine guns.

Senior officers within the *Regia Aeronautica* and Italian Prime Minister Benito Mussolini had become increasingly aware of this technical inferiority as Italy prepared for war, and despite them urging both Fiat and Alfa Romeo to design more powerful radial engines, nothing materialised. As a result of this failure, the General Staff of the *Regia Aeronautica* was forced to ask Italy's German ally for a more powerful

C.202 prototype MM445 was rolled out unpainted, bar pre-war green, white and red rudder markings that also included the House of Savoy crest. The aircraft made its maiden flight from Lonate Pozzolo on 10 August 1940 with Macchi test pilot Guido Carestiato at the controls (*Maurizio Di Terlizzi Collection*)

Legendary Macchi test pilot Guido Carestiato performed the maiden flights of both the *Folgore* and *Veltro* protoypes in August 1940 and April 1942, respectively. On 24 October 1942, he attacked an RAF Lancaster of No 5 Group during a daylight raid on Milan while flying C.202 MM9402. Six years later, while a member of the Macchi mission to Egypt, he tested the C.205Vs delivered to the REAF (*Author's Collection*)

The C.200 *Saetta* would provide the foundation for Dr Mario Castoldi's C.202. Although the aircraft was a joy to fly (like the majority of Italian fighters in World War 2) thanks to it being highly manoeuvrable and light on the controls, the C.200 was both underpowered and under-armed (*Tony Holmes Collection*)

engine in the form of the tried and tested Daimler-Benz DB 601, as fitted to the Bf 109E.

Accordingly, an agreement was reached for Alfa Romeo to licence-build the V12 1175 hp liquid-cooled DB 601A-1 as the RA.1000 RC41-I *Monsone* (Monsoon). The first six DB 601s had been delivered to the *Regia Aeronautica* by late 1939, with two being allotted to Macchi in Varese, in the Lombardy region of northern Italy. One of these engines was fitted to a slightly modified C.200 airframe, with the resulting fighter being designated the C.202, later named *Folgore* (Lightning).

Designed by engineer Mario Castoldi, the 'new' fighter was 60 mph faster than the C.200 thanks to the combination of increased power from the DB 601 and improved streamlining from its smaller frontal area. The C.202 also had an enclosed cockpit and slightly modified wings. Macchi test pilot Guido Carestiato subsequently commented positively on these aspects of the aircraft after completing prototype MM445's maiden flight from Macchi's facility at Lonate Pozzolo on 10 August 1940. Aside from boasting a top speed of 372 mph, the aircraft could also climb to an altitude of 20,000 ft in around six minutes and cruise at 37,500 ft – the C.200 could not exceed 29,200 ft.

In September the C.202 was ordered into series production, with three manufacturers – Macchi, Breda and SAI Ambrosini – receiving contracts in an effort to accelerate deliveries to frontline units. Macchi duly supplied its first aircraft to the *Regia Aeronautica* on 30 June 1941, with Breda following suite on 2 October and SAI Ambrosini 18 days later.

4° *Stormo*'s 9° *Gruppo* was the first unit to be issued with C.202s, with *Serie I* production aircraft being delivered to Gorizia, in northeastern Italy. Other units to see combat with the *Folgore* included 1° *Stormo*'s 6° *Gruppo*, 4° *Stormo*'s 10° *Gruppo*, 51° *Stormo*'s 155° and 20° *Gruppi*, 3° *Stormo*'s 23° *Gruppo*, 150° and 21° *Gruppi Autonomi*, 53° *Stormo*'s 151° and 153° *Gruppi*, 54° *Stormo*'s 16° and 7° *Gruppi*, 154° and 24° *Gruppi Autonomi*, 3° *Stormo*'s 18° *Gruppo*, 22° *Gruppo Autonomo*, 2° *Stormo*'s

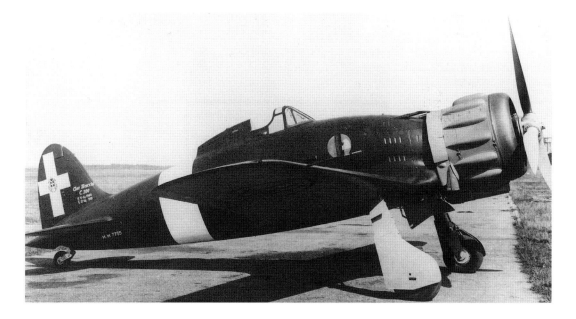

13° *Gruppo* (which received aircraft from 4° *Stormo*) and 161° *Gruppo Autonomo*, which also received used C.202s from other units. Altogether, the three companies produced 13 series of C.202s totalling almost 1300 *Folgores* (392 by Macchi, and the balance split between Breda and SAI Ambrosini) over three years.

C.202s saw widespread service, quickly demonstrating a marked superiority over the Tomahawk, Kittyhawk, Hurricane I/II and Fulmar in North Africa and the Mediterranean. However, the *Folgore* met its match with the Spitfire VB/C, although experienced pilots could often hold their own in combat with the RAF's best fighter.

During 1942, the C.202 was the *Regia Aeronautica*'s 'star' in North Africa, with *Folgore* pilots scoring most of the aerial victories credited to the *Regia Aeronautica* that year. From that peak, the fortunes of C.202 units rapidly declined with the growth of Allied air power in-theatre. From the autumn of 1942 Italian fighter units were increasingly opposed by squadrons flying Spitfire IXs, P-38 Lightnings and P-40K/L Warhawks. All three types had equal or better performance than the *Folgore*, were more heavily armed and were in service in appreciably larger numbers.

Although aerial combat over North Africa and the Mediterranean had highlighted the strong points of the C.202 (speed, agility and

The clean and compact engine installation of the DB 601 in the C.202 gave the fighter a very small frontal area, just as it did in the Bf 109. Unsurprisingly, the *Folgore*'s forged magnesium alloy cantilever engine mounting was also very similar to the one used in the Messerschmitt fighter (*Tony Holmes Collection*)

Factory-fresh *Serie III* C.202 MM7762 was one of 140 *Folgores* constructed by Macchi between May 1941 and April 1942. Production examples differed from the prototype by having indentations in the headrest fairing for improved rear vision, a fixed tailwheel and a long supercharger intake (*Tony Holmes Collection*)

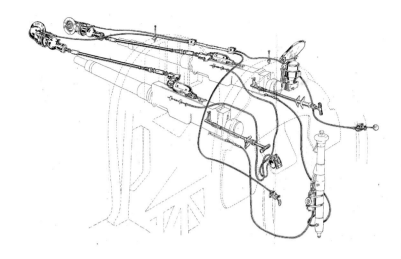

Boasting just two Breda-SAFAT 12.7mm machine guns, the C.202 was one of the mostly lightly armed fighters of World War 2. To make matters worse, both guns were synchronised to fire through the propeller arc, reducing the weapons' rate of fire. The latter would vary from 380 up to 750 rounds per minute, depending on the speed at which the propeller was rotating (*Tony Holmes Collection*)

The last of Dr Mario Castoldi's long line of Macchi fighters was the C.205, which remained in limited production post-war. The initial DB 605-powered model to appear in prototype form was the C.205N-1 *Orione*, which failed to attain operational service due to the level of redesign involved in its creation. This aircraft (MM499) was one of just two examples built, being flown for the first time on 1 November 1942. The *Orione* had a greater wingspan than the C.202/205V and improved armament (four 12.7 mm machine guns and a single 20 mm cannon) (*Tony Holmes Collection*)

rugged construction), the aircraft's weaknesses had also been exposed. Its wingspan (34 ft 8.5 in) was more than two feet shorter than that of the Spitfire V/IX, and this adversely affected the Macchi's performance at altitudes in excess of 20,000 ft – the height at which aerial engagements routinely took place. The aircraft's radio also proved to be so unreliable that pilots preferred to rely on hand gestures instead. There had been problems with the undercarriage partially lowering following high-g pull-outs, and faulty oxygen systems had plagued early operations with the aircraft. Finally, the C.202's armament had become increasingly ineffective in the face of newer RAF fighters armed with 20 mm cannon.

The *Folgore* had initially entered service fitted with just two cowling-mounted Breda-SAFAT 12.7 mm machine guns. This shortcoming was later addressed with the installation of two more machine guns in the wings in *Serie II* through to *VII*. However, in frontline service, these additional weapons were rarely used due to the increased weight associated with their fitment. One series also boasted two 20 mm cannon in underwing gondolas. The provision of an armoured windscreen for *Serie IV* aircraft onward proved more popular with pilots.

As the Mediterranean air war swung decisively in favour of the Allies, large numbers of twin- and four-engined American bombers, escorted by potent new fighter types, began to proliferate in Italian skies. Heavily armed and armoured, the bombers proved almost impossible for *Folgore* pilots to shoot down. Clearly a new, more powerful interceptor was required.

Mario Castoldi had in fact been working on two such aircraft since December 1941. The first of these was the C.205N (subsequently named

Orione), which, because of the level of redesign involved in its creation, would never reach operational service. The second fighter, which married the outstanding 1475 hp Daimler-Benz DB 605A-1 engine with the C.200 wing and C.202 fuselage aft of the engine firewall, was chosen due to the speed in which it could enter service. Initially designated the C.202bis, it would soon become the C.205V *Veltro* (Greyhound).

Aside from its new engine, the *Serie I Veltro* was to be armed with two 12.7 mm machine guns in the nose (each with 370 rounds per weapon) and two more machine guns of this calibre in the wings (with 500 rounds each). The last aircraft in this initial production series (completed in June 1943) had two German-built 20 mm

Macchi designer Mario Castoldi poses in front of a C.205V in 1943. He had gained fame in the 1920s for his world speed record-setting seaplanes which competed successfully in the Schneider Trophy (*Tony Holmes Collection*)

MG 151 Mauser cannon in the wings (with 250 rounds per gun). Wing cannon were subsequently a common feature of *Serie III* aircraft.

The *Veltro* differed from the *Folgore* in other areas too, including the employment of twin barrel-shaped oil radiators to allow better air flow to the coolant radiator, and a new spinner and propeller. New-build C.205Vs also had a more aerodynamic, retractable tailwheel, while C.202s modified into *Veltros* kept the fixed tailwheel.

The first DB 605A-1 reached Italy from Germany in February 1942, and it was installed in *Serie IX* C.202 MM9487. The C.205V's performances proved to be startling from the word go, with Lonate Pozzolo carrying out the prototype's maiden flight on 14 April 1942. The improvement in the rate of climb (it could reach an altitude of 20,000 ft in around five minutes) and top speed (399 mph) were noted by the test pilots that flew MM9487, although they also detected a moderate loss of manoeuvrability above 20,000 ft.

From 10 May the aircraft was rigorously tested at Guidonia airfield near Rome, with Generale Guglielmo Cassinelli climbing to 26,200 ft and attaining a top speed of 404.2 mph at this altitude. He also managed to reach 20,000 ft in 4 min and 52 sec. A second prototype (MM9488) soon followed, with Colonnello Angelo Tondi taking the fighter aloft for the first time on 19 August 1942. Powered by Fiat's licence-built version of the DB 605A, designated the RA.1050 RC58 *Tifone* (Typhoon), the fighter had a slightly inferior performance to MM9487 due to it being 88 lbs heavier.

Castoldi's deliberate decision to employ as much of the C.202 airframe as possible in the C.205V meant production aircraft could be delivered by Macchi to the *Regia Aeronautica* from October 1942, just six months after the prototype's first flight. However, a chronic shortage of parts and

Generale Guglielmo Cassinelli test-flew *Veltro* prototype MM9487 from Guidonia in May 1942, during which time he pushed the prototype to a top speed of 404.2 mph at 26,000 ft (*Author's Collection*)

Serie IX C.202 MM9487 served as the prototype for the C.205V, with the aircraft being taken aloft – from Lonate Pozzolo – for the first time on 14 April 1942. Two of the *Veltro*'s key recognition features are visible in this view, namely the blunt propeller and twin cylindrical oil coolers below the exhaust stubs (*Maurizio Di Terlizzi Collection*)

strategic materials following a series of devastating night raids by RAF Bomber Command on industrial targets in Milan, Turin and Genoa from the autumn of 1942 through to mid-August 1943 meant Fiat struggled to build 12 engines per month at its Turin plant.

Fiat was also supposed to build *Serie II* C.205Vs, but these aircraft never materialised because the company stated that it was too busy developing the G.55 *Centauro* fighter – a contemporary of the *Veltro*. Altogether, Macchi had produced just 100 *Serie I* and 77 *Serie III* aircraft by the time the Armistice between Italy and Allied armed forces came into effect on 8 September 1943.

Despite its paucity in numbers, the C.205V was fondly remembered by Italian pilots who were fortunate enough to fly it. High-scoring ace Maresciallo Luigi Gorrini flew the fighter with the pro-German *Aeronautica Repubblicana* (AR) following the Armistice, and he stated that it 'was the most beautiful aircraft I flew into combat during the war, being appreciated and envied by the Germans and feared by the enemy'.

As noted by Gorrini, the Allies also respected the C.205V. Lt Cdr Eric Brown, Chief Naval Test Pilot and CO of the Captured Enemy Aircraft Flight, evaluated a *Veltro* shortly after VE Day. He too was fulsome in his praise of the fighter;

'One of the finest aircraft I ever flew was the Macchi C.205. Here you had the perfect combination of Italian styling and German engineering. I believe it was powered by a Daimler-Benz DB 605. It was really a delight to fly, and up to anything on the Allied programme. But again, it came just before the Italians capitulated, so it was never used extensively. We did tests on it and were most impressed. The cockpit was smallish, but not as bad as the Bf 109.'

CHAPTER TWO

FOLGORES OVER MALTA

A s noted in the previous chapter, the first fighter unit to receive C.202s was C.200-equipped 9° *Gruppo*, followed shortly thereafter by 6° *Gruppo* (it too replaced C.200s with *Folgores*). They were part of the elite 4° and 1° *Stormi Caccia Terrestre*, respectively. *Serie I* and *II* C.202s were delivered to 9° *Gruppo* at Gorizia from 30 June through to early August 1941, with pilots quickly transitioning to the aircraft.

On 24 September, 31 *Folgores* of 9° *Gruppo* departed Gorizia for Comiso, near Ragusa on Sicily. During the unit's long journey south, its C.202s made a brief stopover at Rome-Ciampino Sud airport so that they could be reviewed by Prime Minister Benito Mussolini on 29 September. Later that same day, 9° *Gruppo*, led by *stormo* CO, Colonnello Eugenio Leotta, reached Comiso. Within 24 hours of their arrival, the C.202 pilots would have the opportunity to test their mettle against the seasoned Hurricane-equipped fighter force on Malta.

On 30 September, shortly after 1100 hrs, 11 Hurricane IIs of Malta-based No 185 Sqn targeted Comiso airfield. Three C.202s of 9° *Gruppo*'s 97ᵃ *Squadriglia* were scrambled to intercept them, the *Folgores* being flown by Tenente Luigi Tessari, future ace Sottotenente Jacopo Frigerio and Sergente Maggiore Massimo Salvatore. Five of the attackers were 'Hurri-bombers', each armed with six 40-lb bombs and two 25-lb incendiaries, and they made a single pass over the airfield at low level while the six remaining fighters provided top cover.

An impressive line-up of 31 C.202s from 4° *Stormo*'s 9° *Gruppo* await inspection by Prime Minister Benito Mussolini at Rome-Ciampino Sud airport on 29 September. The fighters were on their way south to Sicily, from where they would join the fight to subjugate Malta (*Aeronautica Militare-Fototeca Storica*)

Sottotenente Jacopo Frigerio of 9° *Gruppo's* 97ª *Squadriglia* was the first pilot to claim a victory with a C.202, downing a 'Hurri-bomber' from No 185 Sqn just north of Gozo on 30 September 1941. Having survived the war, Frigerio would lose his life in October 1955 when the engine in the USAF F-86D he was flying on a training mission from Nellis AFB, Nevada, failed. He tried to glide the fighter back to base, but crashed short of the runway (*Author's Collection*)

Having expended their bombs, the enemy aircraft headed for home, although they were soon chased down by the appreciably faster C.202s. Sottotenente Frigerio shot down the 'Hurri-bomber' of Plt Off D W Lintern, who was seen bailing out just north of Gozo. After returning home and hastily refuelling, five of the Hurricanes got airborne once again to escort a Royal Navy Fulmar of the Kalafrana Rescue Flight that was tasked with locating the downed pilot for possible retrieval by one of the flight's Swordfish floatplanes.

This rescue force then encountered more C.202s from 97ª *Squadriglia* as they patrolled the area. Although not a single Hurricane was damaged in the brief engagement, the Fulmar was effectively targeted by Tenente Luigi Tessari and Maresciallo Raffaello Novelli, who claimed it shot down. The doomed aircraft ditched and its crew managed to clamber into their dinghy, and they were subsequently rescued by a Swordfish floatplane. No trace of Plt Off Lintern was ever found.

During the clash with the Fulmar, Tenente Tessari's *Folgore* had been bounced by future ace Flt Lt Charles 'Porky' Jeffries, and he holed it so severely that he claimed the aircraft as a probable kill. Trailing smoke, the Italian fighter managed to land back at Comiso.

On 1 October, 9° *Gruppo* undertook its first operation over Malta, during which six C.202s from 73ª *Squadriglia*, led by *squadriglia* CO Capitano Mario Pluda, fought with eight Hurricanes from No 185 Sqn 30 miles northeast of the island. The latter had scrambled at 1150 hrs to intercept the approaching intruders, only to be bounced by the Macchis whilst they were still climbing to 24,000 ft. Although squadron CO, and Battle of France ace, Sqn Ldr Peter 'Boy' Mould was shot down and killed, Sgt Ernie Knight got in amongst the *Folgores* and damaged one of them. His victim was Capitano Carlo Ivaldi, whose C.202 was hit in its main fuel tank. After running out of fuel, Ivaldi was compelled to force-land his damaged *Folgore* on a Sicilian beach near Pozzallo.

Along with Ivaldi, Tenente Piero Bonfatti and Sergente Maggiore Enrico Dallari each claimed a Hurricane shot down and two shared probables on their first pass. Only Mould was lost, however.

No 185 Sqn suffered another loss to C.202s on 4 October, when two Hurricanes took off to identify six bandits. Although no contact with the enemy apparently took place, Plt Off Peter Veitch was killed when he crashed off Benghaisa Point. The aircraft was almost certainly attacked by Sergente Teresio Martinoli, who claimed a Hurricane destroyed that day.

Following ten days of little activity for 9° *Gruppo*, just before dawn on 14 October six C.202s led by 96ª *Squadriglia* CO Capitano Ezio Viglione Borghese strafed Luqa airfield. Five Malta Night Fighter Unit (MNFU) Hurricanes scrambled, followed by three Hurricanes each from Nos 126 and 185 Sqns. Once engaged with the C.202s, Plt Off David Barnwell of the MNFU Hurricane jumped the *Folgore* of Tenente Emanuele Annoni and holed its rear fuselage with two 20 mm shells. Annoni was distracted by a jammed machine gun when he was attacked, Barnwell radioing 'Tally-ho! Tally-ho! Got one! Got one!' as he fired at the C.202.

Having just claimed his fifth success to 'make ace', Barnwell (the MNFU's most successful pilot at this time) was bounced by Sottotenente Bruno Paolazzi, who shot the Hurricane off Annoni's tail. Five minutes later, Barnwell radioed 'Bailing out, engine cut – am coming down in the sea'. No sign of Barnwell was subsequently found. Annoni managed to make it back to base, while Paolazzi and Maresciallo Manlio Olivetti claimed two Hurricanes shot down.

On 19 October, five 'Hurri-bombers' from No 126 Sqn, escorted by Hurricanes from No 249 Sqn, attacked Comiso airfield. As they raced for home, the RAF fighters were bounced by six C.202s from 9° *Gruppo*'s 73ᵃ *Squadriglia*. The Hurricane flown by Sgt Dave Owen of No 249 Sqn was damaged in the ensuing action, although he managed to nurse his fighter back to Malta. Sergente Teresio Martinoli claimed two Hurricane kills.

C.202s and Hurricanes next clashed at 1755 hrs on 22 October, when 14 *Folgores* from 9° *Gruppo* (led by Tenente Colonnello Marco Minio Paluello) targeted Luqa airfield. While six fighters from 73ᵃ *Squadriglia* made a strafing pass, the remaining eight C.202s flew top cover. The latter attacked nine Hurricanes from No 249 Sqn as they climbed to intercept the Italian fighters, Sgt Dave Owen's 'GN-R' being shot down in flames (its pilot bailed out) and Plt Off Bob Matthews' fighter also being hit. The C.202 pilots grossly overclaimed when they returned to base, being credited with seven victories and two probables. Among those to enjoy success was Sergente Teresio Martinoli, who recorded his fourth confirmed kill of the month.

4° *Stormo* suffered its first combat loss of a C.202 on 25 October during an escort mission for four Z.1007bis from 9° *Stormo* BT targeting shipping in Grand Harbour. The bombers had been supplied with direct escort by C.200s from 54° *Stormo*, and 20 C.202s from 9° *Gruppo* provided indirect support.

Eight No 185 Sqn Hurricanes were scrambled to intercept the bombers, and they dived on the formation around midday. Moments after firing on the bombers, the Hurricanes were jumped by the C.202s and Sgt Ernest Knight was shot down. In return, Sgt Cyril Hunton downed the C.202 of 4° *Stormo* commander Colonnello Eugenio Leotta. The fighter was seen leaving the area trailing black smoke, and Hunton was credited with a probable kill. Shortly thereafter, wreckage was found floating in the sea by an Italian search craft. Leotta, whose body was never recovered, posthumously received a *Medaglia d'Oro al Valor Militare*. The remaining C.202 pilots claimed three Hurricanes destroyed, with one being credited to Capitano Antonio Larsimont Pergameni and the others shared between Capitano Mario Pluda and Tenente Piero Bonfatti.

During the first week of November, C.202s from 9° *Gruppo* engaged RAF fighters and bombers on several occasions. On the 1st, six Blenheim IVs from Nos 18 and 107 Sqns were intercepted by 12 *Folgores* while they attacked an Axis convoy. Sergenti Teresio Martinoli and Mario Guerci each claimed a bomber

Tenente Emanuele Annoni of 9° *Gruppo*'s 96ᵃ *Squadriglia* would end the war with nine victories to his name. Nicknamed 'il Cardinale' ('the cardinal'), he was known for his calm, authoritative and poised personality. On 14 October 1941 his C.202 (MM7742 96-8) was shot up in combat over Malta, although Annoni returned to Sicily unscathed. His unit was transferred to Libya shortly thereafter, and he was credited with an early *Folgore* victory in this theatre on 26 November 1941 (*Author's Collection*)

The first Italian unit to see combat with the C.202 was 97ᵃ *Squadriglia*, 9° *Gruppo*, 4° *Stormo*. One of the first fighters issued to the *Stormo* was this Serie III aircraft, MM7735 97-5 (which lacks a dust filter). Based at Comiso, on Sicily, from late September 1941, this particular fighter would engage RAF Hurricane IIs over Malta on a number of occasions (*Tony Holmes Collection*)

Colonnello Eugenio Leotta, who had led 4° *Stormo* since 5 May 1941, was killed on 25 October 1941 when his C.202 (MM7728) was shot down over Malta by No 185 Sqn Hurricane IIs. His *Folgore* was the first confirmed C.202 victory for the island's Hurricane force (*USSMA*)

destroyed, although none were in fact lost. The Blenheim crews stated that the Italian fighters 'failed to press home their attacks'. A bomber was damaged, and Tenente Felice Bussolin was shot down by one of the Blenheims.

The following day, three C.202s were scrambled after aircraft were detected approaching Sicily. They found nothing, and were on short finals to land back at Comiso when the alarm sounded again and two of the fighters headed off in the direction of nearby Gela. Here, they sighted a Wellington from the Overseas Aircraft Delivery Unit being ferried from Gibraltar to Malta. The aircraft was duly shot down by a number of fighters that had converged on the area.

After a short lull in the action, on the 8th a fierce combat unfolded over Malta at midday when 18 *Folgores* from 4° *Stormo*, led by Tenente Colonnello Marco Minio Paluello, and a similar number of C.200s from 54° *Stormo*, escorted four Z.1007bis. The formation was intercepted by four Hurricanes of No 126 Sqn led by ace Flt Lt J M V 'Chips' Carpenter, who claimed a C.202 shot down. Sgt Allan Haley's Hurricane collided with a C.202, which broke up in the air, while the RAF fighter crashed near an anti-aircraft gun emplacement west of Zebbug after Haley bailed out. Plt Off Patrick Lardner-Burke claimed another C.202 shot down, giving him ace status.

Having damaged a second *Folgore* minutes later, Lardner-Burke was in turn badly wounded when a 12.7 mm round fired from a 96ª *Squadriglia* C.202 at close range penetrated the armour plate behind his seat and passed through his chest, puncturing a lung. Despite this, Lardner-Burke managed to land back at base, where he was immediately hospitalised.

4° *Stormo* had indeed lost two C.202s in this action, Capitano Mario Pluda (the CO of 73ª *Squadriglia*) colliding with Sgt Haley's Hurricane and Sergente Maggiore Luigi Taroni falling to Flt Lt Carpenter. The Italians claimed just one shared kill in return, credited to several 96ª *Squadriglia* pilots, plus two Hurricanes damaged.

On 12 November 11 'Hurri-bombers' drawn from Nos 126 and 249 Sqns headed for Comiso, escorted by ten Hurricane fighters from these units. They were engaged by three C.202s from 9° *Gruppo* that had been scrambled a short while earlier when three Hurricanes had strafed Gela as a precursor to the Comiso attack. Sottotenente Giovanni Deanna and Sergente Maggiore Massimo Salvatore shot down the 'Hurri-bomber' flown by No 126 Sqn's Sgt Peter Simpson, who ditched into the sea. He was rescued shortly thereafter by an Italian launch.

By the time C.202s next engaged the enemy over the Mediterranean, a second *Folgore*-equipped unit in the form of 17° *Gruppo* had been sent to Comiso. However, unlike 9° *Gruppo*, it would remain on Sicily for just a week before flying on to Cyrenaica, in Libya, in response to Operation *Crusader*, launched by the Allies on 18 November. Attached to 1° *Stormo*, 17° *Gruppo* had commenced its conversion onto the aircraft from the C.200 when, on 2 October 1941, the first five Breda-built *Folgores* were delivered to 71ª *Squadriglia* at Campoformido airfield, in northern Italy. Within three weeks the *squadriglia* had received its full complement of ten C.202s.

By late October, 34 Breda- and Macchi-built fighters had been sent to Campoformido, where they were divided up between 71ª, 72ª and

80ª *Squadriglie*. Pilots trained on the C.202s until 28 October, when 17° *Gruppo* was ordered to Rome. Two days later, the unit was inspected by *Generale d'Armata* Ugo Cavallero, Armed Forces Chief of General Staff, and *Generale di Squadra Aerea* Francesco Pricolo, the *Regia Aeronautica*'s Chief of Staff.

The *gruppo* remained at Rome-Ciampino for three weeks while sand filters were fitted to the aircraft and light hazelnut mottles were applied over the fighters' dark olive green uppersurfaces. Finally, on 18 November, 71ª *Squadriglia* was ready to continue its journey south. With the *Folgore*'s maximum range being a modest 475 miles, it was necessary to make two refuelling stops along the route. The unit initially landed at Naples-Capodichino and then overnighted at Reggio Calabria, before pressing on to Comiso the following day.

During the afternoon of 21 November, 71ª *Squadriglia*'s Sergente Remo Broilo claimed the unit's first victory with the C.202. The day's action had begun several hours earlier when six *Folgores* from 9° *Gruppo* had intercepted a lone Hurricane II undertaking a photo-reconnaissance mission over Sicily. The aircraft, flown by Wg Cdr John Dowland (the CO of No 69 Sqn), was shot down by Sergente Alfredo Bombardini. Dowland bailed out, and he was rescued by a Kalafrana-based Swordfish floatplane.

Whilst Dowland was attempting to reconnoitre Sicily, five C.200s of 54ª *Squadriglia* and ten C.202s from 97ª *Squadriglia* strafed Hal Far airfield. The C.200s were intercepted by seven Hurricanes from No 185 Sqn, while the RAF fighters were in turn bounced by the *Folgores*. The Italian pilots claimed four Hurricanes shot down and one Blenheim damaged on the ground. In reality, only Sgt Bill Nurse's Hurricane had been damaged, albeit badly. Two 'Spitfires' were also supposedly shot down, the aircraft being shared between five pilots – Sottotenente Jacopo Frigerio, Maresciallo Raffaello Novelli and Sergente Maggiore Massimo Salvatore.

Eighteen C.202s returned to strafe in the afternoon. Although most of these aircraft were from 9° *Gruppo*, several of the fighters belonged to 71ª *Squadriglia*. The *Folgores* were intercepted by four Hurricanes from No 185 Sqn that had been on a convoy patrol. The Italians subsequently claimed five victories, with Capitano Antonio Larsimont Pergameni, Maresciallo Raffaello Novelli and Sergente Remo Broilo being amongst the victorious pilots. Only one Hurricane failed to return, with its pilot, Sgt Dick Cousens, being lost.

The next day, 21 Hurricanes from Nos 126 and 249 Sqns were led aloft by Wing Commander Takali, high-scoring ace Wg Cdr Sandy Rabagliati, after a large raid was detected. The latter comprised ten Italian Ju 87s from 101° *Gruppo Tuffatori*, escorted by 61 C.200s and C.202s. Although the close escort C.200s returned early, the C.202s, providing indirect cover, were intercepted by the Hurricanes. The *Folgore* pilots later claimed to have engaged '40' fighters, and they were credited with eight 'Spitfires' destroyed. Not a single Hurricane was, in fact, lost, and 9° *Gruppo* had Tenente Piero Bonfatti killed.

This action proved to be the last involving large numbers of C.202s over Malta in 1941, for the Luftwaffe now increased its strength in the Mediterranean with the posting of *Luftflotte* 2 to the theatre from the Eastern Front due to the onset of winter weather in the Soviet Union. This in turn

A pilot from 90ª *Squadriglia*, 10° *Gruppo*, 4° *Stormo* is helped by groundcrew into C.202 MM7810 90-3 at Gela prior to flying a mission to Malta in April 1942. The individual on the extreme left appears to be holding seatback armour in his right hand. This aircraft was transferred to North Africa shortly after this photograph was taken, and it was one of two C.202s from 10° *Gruppo* destroyed (with six more damaged) in an Allied bombing raid on Martuba on 28 May 1942 (*Archivio Ufficio Storico Stato Maggiore Esercito-Archivio Fotografico*)

allowed the *Regia Aeronautica* to send most of the Sicily-based C.202s to North Africa from 23 November to evaluate the non-tropicalised aircraft in desert conditions.

On that date, 9° *Gruppo*'s 96ª and 97ª *Squadriglie* were sent to Martuba, with 17° *Gruppo* following suit two days later. 9° *Gruppo*'s 73ª *Squadriglia* would remain on Sicily, however, the unit's handful of pilots being tasked with flying photo-reconnaissance missions over Malta with camera-equipped C.202s. Its efforts would be supported by a photographic section from 7° *Gruppo*'s C.200-equipped 86ª *Squadriglia* (the flight was also equipped with two C.202s passed on to it by 9° *Gruppo*), based on nearby Pantelleria.

Amongst the photo-reconnaissance pilots to distinguish themselves in Maltese skies was 86ª *Squadriglia*'s Sottotenente Don Gabriele Ferretti di Castelferretto. A young nobleman fighter pilot who performed several successful lone reconnaissance sorties in the *Folgore*, he lost his life on 5 December when his C.202 dived into the ground on Sicily from a height of 26,000 ft upon returning from a sortie to Malta. The cause of his demise remained a mystery, although a faulty oxygen system seems the most likely culprit. He was subsequently awarded a posthumous *Medaglia d'Oro al Valor Militare*.

Thirteen days later, future ace and figurehead of the AR, Tenente Adriano Visconti, joined 86ª *Squadriglia*. He duly flew a number of photo-reconnaissance missions over Malta, and during one of these (on 22 December) he was pursued by the No 249 Sqn Hurricane flown by Plt Off Robert Matthews. Visconti made good his escape when Matthews was shot down and killed by Bf 109s from I./JG 53.

For almost four months the skies over Malta had been all but devoid of Italian aircraft, as Luftwaffe units shouldered the burden of the offensive against the beleaguered island. This was about to change, for at sunset on 2 April 1942 4° *Stormo* returned to Sicily when recently re-equipped 10° *Gruppo* (led by Capitano Franco Lucchini) flew 26 C.202s to Castelvetrano. 9° *Gruppo* followed suit on 15 April. The *Aeronautica della Sicilia* now had a powerful force at its disposal, ready to support the Luftwaffe in the spring campaign against Malta.

On 19 April 54° *Stormo* received a small number of photo-reconnaissance C.202RFs for 7° *Gruppo*'s 76ª *Squadriglia*. These aircraft, equipped with Kodak 30 cm cameras, routinely flew lone missions over Malta from Castelvetrano and Pantelleria airfields.

That same day, 10° *Gruppo* had performed an acclimatisation flight over Malta – the RAF fighter force was at such a low ebb they had been unable to oppose such missions since 14 April. During the course of the operation, Sergente Elio Trevisan of 90ª *Squadriglia* was forced to bail out of his C.202 when the fighter's oxygen system failed. This would prove to be a recurring problem for Sicily-based C.202s in 1942.

On 20 April 19 *Folgores* from 10° *Gruppo* were again tasked with flying a sweep over Malta, the fighters being led by 90ª *Squadriglia* CO Capitano Giovanni Guiducci. However, 30 minutes into the mission, Guiducci and his wingman Sergente Maggiore Giovan Battista Ceoletta collided, and both Macchis crashed into the sea off the Sicilian town of Porto Empedocle. Ceoletta bailed out and was rescued by a fishing boat, but Guiducci was killed. He was replaced by Capitano Ranieri Piccolomini.

At 1645 hrs the following day, the C.202 and Spitfire VB clashed for the first time, Supermarine fighters having been flown in to Malta from Allied aircraft carriers on 2 March and 20 April. The Luftwaffe had sent three large raids against the island during the course of the day, and 22 C.202s from 10° *Gruppo* participated in the last of these attacks. The Italian fighters dived on Spitfires from No 249 Sqn that had in turn been pursuing Bf 109s, and Tenente Luigi Giannella became separated from the rest of the formation during this manoeuvre. He then stated that he was attacked in error by German fighters, although he managed to evade them. Moments later, he spotted five Spitfires and claimed to have shot one down.

The next action involving C.202s took place on 27 April when 27 aircraft from 10° *Gruppo* escorted five Z.1007bis from 50° *Gruppo* targeting vessels in the Grand Harbour. Again, the RAF's fighter strength had been so badly reduced that the raid took place unopposed. Two days later, 10° *Gruppo* escorted five Z.1007bis on an evening attack on Luqa airfield. This time, the aircraft of 73ª *Squadriglia* CO Capitano Aldo Gon was hit by anti-aircraft fire that tracked the formation across the island. The C.202 was badly damaged and Gon seriously wounded, although he managed to return to Sicily and force-land. Tenente Giuseppe Oblach assumed command of the *squadriglia*.

During the late afternoon of 30 April more than 20 C.202s from 10° *Gruppo* escorted four Z.1007bis from 50° *Gruppo* in another raid, and although six Spitfires were scrambled, the Italian aircraft were not intercepted. A similar-sized formation sortied from Sicily 24 hours later, although this time the 19 *Folgores* came from 9° *Gruppo*. Spitfires sent to oppose the Italian aircraft were bounced by Bf 109s, and the only damage inflicted on the C.202s came from anti-aircraft fire – two *Folgores* were slightly damaged. 10° *Gruppo* was again in action on 2 May when it helped Bf 109s escort Ju 88s attacking Luqa and Safi. The following day, 16 C.202s from 9° *Gruppo* covered German Ju 87s targeting Hal Far and Luqa.

On the afternoon of 4 May, five Z.1007bis from 50° *Gruppo*, escorted by five C.202s from 9° *Gruppo* and ten Bf 109s, were intercepted over the Grand Harbour by four Spitfires from No 601 Sqn. In the brief action that followed, the radiator in Sgt Jack McConnell's fighter was holed by Sottotenente Alvaro Querci and Sergente Teresio Martinoli of 73ª *Squadriglia* and he had to crash land his Spitfire at Luqa.

Following yet more uneventful close escort missions for Z.1007bis on 6 and 7 May, C.202s clashed with RAF fighters again during the morning

Maresciallo Pietro del Turco of 10° *Gruppo*'s 90ª *Squadriglia* poses in his flying gear at Gela airfield in May 1942 during 4° *Stormo*'s second operational tour over Malta. Amongst the aircraft lined up in the background is MM7906 90-8, which Tenente Virgilio Vanzan used to share in the destruction of a Kittyhawk I from No 260 Sqn on 12 June 1942. The Macchi was hit by anti-aircraft fire minutes later, although Vanzan made it back to base. Maresciallo Del Turco would be killed in combat with Spitfire VCs from No 92 Sqn over El Alamein on 2 September 1942 (*Archivio Ufficio Storico Stato Maggiore Esercito-Archivio Fotografico*)

of the 8th. On this occasion, six aircraft from 97ª *Squadriglia* were tasked with providing close escort for six Ju 88s from KGr 806 and 15 Ju 87s from III./StG 3, while a further eight fighters from 10° *Gruppo* provided indirect cover. When the bombers were attacked by a mixed formation of Spitfires and Hurricanes, the 97ª *Squadriglia* aircraft, led by Capitano Roberto Dagasso, engaged the Hurricanes of No 185 Sqn that had bounced the Ju 88s. Dagasso and Tenente Ado Bonuti each claimed a kill, although only the Hurricane of ace Sgt 'Tony' Boyd had been hit in the engine and glycol tank. He belly-landed at Takali. Meanwhile, Capitano Franco Lucchini's flight of 10° *Gruppo* aircraft had chased after five 'Spitfires' that were firing at Ju 87s, and Tenente Luigi Giannella was credited with downing two of them.

The C.202 units had, in turn suffered a single casualty when the aircraft of Tenente Giovanni Barcaro from 97ª *Squadriglia* was hit by a 20 mm cannon shell fired by the Hurricane II of No 185 Sqn ace Sgt Wilbert Dodd. The latter reported 'seeing strikes all over' the fighter when he targeted it with a three-second burst from a distance of just 100 yards at an altitude of 17,000 ft. Dodd stated that the aircraft 'turned over and went straight down', and he claimed it as probably destroyed. However, although Barcaro had been wounded in the right arm, he managed to return to base.

C.202s were in action again on 9 May, when they were involved in two raids on Malta. A further 62 Spitfires were also flown in that day from USS *Wasp* (CV-7) and HMS *Eagle*. Although the 16 *Folgores* that participated in the morning raid did not encounter any enemy fighters, an identical number of C.202s (eight each from both 9° and 10° *Gruppi*) escorting the usual five-strong formation of Z.1007bis at 1745 hrs were intercepted by 11 Spitfires from No 126 Sqn. Both sides wildly overclaimed following the engagement, with the Spitfire pilots being credited with three Cants destroyed (none were lost, although one was badly damaged) and the C.202 pilots claiming three Spitfires destroyed and one damaged. All the RAF fighters returned to base unscathed. The only *Folgore* to suffer any damage was the aircraft flown by Tenente Luigi Giannella, which was hit by a solitary 20 mm shell.

Newly equipped 84ª *Squadriglia* shows off its *Serie III* C.202s at Udine airfield in February 1942. At the beginning of April, the unit, as part of 10° *Gruppo*, 4° *Stormo*, was transferred to Castelvetrano airfield on Sicily to support bomber operations against Malta. The stars on the noses of several of the fighters were applied as a unit marking by 84ª *Squadriglia* prior to the adoption of the 4° *F Baracca* signature (*Tony Holmes Collection*)

The following afternoon, at 1810 hrs, five Z.1007bis attacked Malta, escorted by 20 C.202s from 9° *Gruppo* and ten Re.2001s from 2° *Gruppo*. A large force of Spitfires and Hurricanes was scrambled to intercept the raiders, and No 601 Sqn succeeded in downing one Cant and badly damaging two others. A C.202 was also destroyed by Plt Off W A Caldwell, with 97ª *Squadriglia* CO Capitano Roberto Dagasso being killed. In return, the *gruppi* claimed six victories (three were credited to 9° *Gruppo*), although no RAF fighters were lost to the Italian units.

On the afternoon of the 12th, three S.84s from 4° *Gruppo* joined four

Ju 88s in an attack on Takali airfield. They were escorted by 15 Re.2001s from 2° *Gruppo* and 15 C.202s from 9° and 10° *Gruppi*. The formation was set upon by a substantial number of Spitfires and Hurricanes, and Nos 601, 603 and 126 Sqn made multiple claims. The C.202 of 73ª *Squadriglia* pilot Sergente Teresio Martinoli was hit in the tail shortly after he had downed a Spitfire, and Sergente Mario Veronesi of 84ª *Squadriglia* almost certainly damaged the aircraft flown by No 126 Sqn's Flt Sgt C F Bush, who was about to finish off a damaged S.84.

A midday raid by three Ju 88s on Takali on 14 May was escorted by Bf 109s, as well as Re.2001s from 2° *Gruppo* and C.202s from 9° *Gruppo*. RAF fighters from four squadrons opposed the attack, and No 185 Sqn Spitfires engaged the Italian escorts. One C.202 was hit by Flt Sgt D L Ferraby and it fell away trailing smoke, while Flt Sgt 'Tony' Boyd was killed when his Spitfire was shot down by Maresciallo Rinaldo Damiani of 97ª *Squadriglia*.

The following morning, 30 C.202s from both 9° and 10° *Gruppi* escorted three S.84bis targeting St Paul's Bay. Twelve Spitfires from Nos 249 and 603 Sqns attacked the Italian aircraft, and although the bombers escaped unscathed, Flt Sgt L A Verroll shot down the C.202 flown by 91ª *Squadriglia* CO, Capitano Alberto Argenton, who was killed. He was the third *squadriglia* commander that 4° *Stormo* had lost in less than a month. The C.202 pilots in turn claimed four Spitfires shot down, but none had been seriously hit.

An identical number was claimed by 9° *Gruppo* on 16 May when five Z.1007bis were targeted by Nos 601 and 603 Sqns. Two kills were credited to Sergente Maggiore Massimo Salvatore and one each to Sottotenente Mario Squarcina and Maresciallo Rinaldo Damiani. A solitary fighter from No 603 Sqn had been shot up and its pilot, Flt Sgt F R Johnson, forced to crash-land. No other losses were recorded by the RAF.

On the 18th five C.202s from 4° *Stormo* reconnoitred Malta, but Sottotenente Vincenzo Fischer's fighter suffered engine problems en route and turned back early. He was killed while trying to force-land at Gela. Fischer would be the final casualty suffered by 9° or 10° *Gruppi* whilst flying from Sicily. The following day 13 C.202s from 10° *Gruppo* participated in the unit's last raid on Malta when they helped escort three Z.1007bis targeting Luqa and Safi. All three bombers were hit by Spitfires, with one Cant being shot down. A C.202 was also claimed as damaged, but it returned to Sicily.

Between 21–24 May, 4° *Stormo* was transferred to North Africa – for a third time – as the *Regia Aeronautica* strengthened its force in Libya. 51° *Stormo* soon took its place, with 33 brand new C.202s of 155° *Gruppo*

Six C.202s from 91ª *Squadriglia*, 10° *Gruppo*, 4° *Stormo* have their engines run up at Gela prior to commencing their take off runs at the start of a bomber escort mission in April 1942. The second *Folgore* is MM7902, which was damaged in the devastating attack on Martuba on 28 May 1942 (*Archivio Ufficio Storico Stato Maggiore Esercito-Archivio Fotografico*)

C.202 MM7795 90-4 was the regular mount of five-victory ace Sergente Maggiore Amleto Monterumici of 90ª *Squadriglia*, 10° *Gruppo*, 4° *Stormo*. It is seen here with its engine idling at Gela in May 1942. Due to the short distance (60 miles) between Sicily and Malta, most C.202 pilots would fly their aircraft without a full fuel load. The trade-off was better performance once in aerial combat. Monterumici often flew as wingman to high-scoring ace Capitano Franco Lucchini (*Tony Holmes Collection*)

being deployed from Rome-Ciampino to Gela at the end of May. It would soon tangle with Malta's defenders.

During the afternoon of 1 June, 155° *Gruppo* CO Maggiore Duilio Fanali led a number of his newly arrived pilots on an uneventful sweep of Malta. The *gruppo* claimed its first success the following morning when 32 C.202s provided indirect escort for three S.84s heading for Safi. The bombers also had more than 20 Re.2001s from 2° *Gruppo* as close escort. Twenty Spitfires were scrambled, and Capitano Carlo Miani of 360ª *Squadriglia* was credited with downing the Spitfire of Plt Off J R Halford from No 185 Sqn – he ditched in Kalafrana Bay.

155° *Gruppo* would escort bombers targeting Malta on a near-daily basis throughout June, and it suffered a handful of losses and was credited with a modest number of victories in return. Again, overclaiming was rife by either side. Perhaps the most significant actual loss recorded that month by the *gruppo* came on the 23rd when 27 C.202s escorted three S.84s heading for Takali. No 603 Sqn intercepted the raid, and Plt Offs D G Newman and Ray Smith singled out the *Folgore* flown by six-victory ace Maresciallo Aldo Buvoli, who later recalled;

'While I was flying in a tight turn, I heard the terrific noise of a burst fired from close range. At that very moment I saw the dark shape of an aircraft overtaking me very fast! I was sure my Macchi was hit! In fact, everything began to vibrate. All efforts to control the aircraft were in vain and then sudden warmth came from under the cockpit. Fire! I unhooked the canopy and bailed out!'

Buvoli was soon captured. His was the only Italian fighter to be downed that day, and 155° *Gruppo* claimed four Spitfires destroyed in return. Just one was lost.

The following day 51° *Stormo*'s 20° *Gruppo*, under the leadership of Maggiore Gino Callieri, reached Gela. The *stormo*'s HQ flight, led by Tenente Colonnello Aldo Remondino, also reached Sicily on the 24th. These units could muster 36 brand new C.202s between them, and their arrival was a precursor to the second major Italian assault on Malta, which would run from 1 to 14 July.

The *Folgore* pilots would be kept busier than ever before during the new offensive, as they shouldered more of the bomber escort role than had previously been the case. German fighter units also remained committed to the campaign, and Axis forces were opposed by four squadrons of Spitfires.

Three separate missions were flown by C.202s on 1 July, with a small number of bombers at around 25,000 ft being escorted by up to 50 fighters flying above and behind them. Such tactics had been employed by the *Regia Aeronautica* over Malta for more than a year. Axis fighter pilots claimed ten Spitfires destroyed, one probable and ten damaged, when only one fighter was in fact destroyed. The No 603 Sqn aircraft of Flt Sgt J H Ballantyne fell to 151ª *Squadriglia*'s Maresciallo Ennio Tarantola. No *Folgores* were lost in return, despite Spitfire pilots claiming four destroyed.

Three C.202s fell to Spitfires the following day during the course of two escort missions. On a more positive note for 51° *Stormo*, its future ranking *Folgore* ace of the Malta campaign, Capitano Furio Niclot Doglio (who was also CO of 151ª *Squadriglia*), claimed his first Spitfire victory – C.202 pilots were credited with four in total. Three RAF fighters crash-landed following encounters with *Folgores*.

The Italian bombers were badly mauled during two raids on 4 July, despite the presence of large numbers of C.202s. Although five Spitfires were reportedly destroyed by the escorting *Folgore* pilots, in reality none had been lost. Two returned to base badly shot up. Two C.202s were, however, destroyed by Spitfires during the course of two raids on the 6th, with one of the aircraft being credited to Sgt George Beurling of No 249 Sqn. The first of eight *Folgores* he would claim destroyed in the defence of Malta, the Canadian, who had 'made ace' during this mission, later recalled;

'As the [Ju 88] bombers turned to run I saw a Macchi 202 boring up on "Smitty's" [Flg Off John Smith] tail. I did a quick climbing turn and bored in [vertically from 20,000 ft down to 5000 ft] on the "Eyetie", catching him unawares. A one-second burst smacked him in the engine and glycol tank. He burst into flames and went down like a plummet.'

Beurling's victim was five-victory ace Sergente Maggiore Francesco Pecchiari of 352ª *Squadriglia*, who was killed. *Folgore* pilots from both 20° and 155° *Gruppi* were credited with three Spitfires destroyed in return, one of which was claimed by Capitano Furio Niclot Doglio. A Spitfire crash-landed with battle damage and Beurling's fighter was badly holed.

Aircraft from both C.202 *gruppi* sortied twice over Malta again on 7 July, and Capitano Furio Niclot Doglio shared in the destruction of a Spitfire with his wingman Maresciallo Ennio Tarantola during the morning raid – two RAF fighters were lost to Axis fighters. Two C.202s were badly shot up in return. The *Folgore* of Tenente Fabrizio Cherubini from 353ª *Squadriglia*

Capitano Furio Niclot Doglio, CO of 151ª *Squadriglia*, 20° *Gruppo*, 51° *Stormo*, poses with his C.202 MM9042 151-1 at Gela in July 1942. His aircraft featured a small chevron on either side of the fuselage, denoting that it was flown by the unit commander. Niclot Doglio scored his last two victories over Malta in this C.202 on 13 July 1942, taking his final tally to 7.5 kills. He perished in MM9042 when he fell victim to Sgt George Beurling on 27 July (*Tony Holmes Collection*)

Italy's second-highest scoring ace over Malta during 1942 was Maresciallo Ennio Tarantola (left), seen here pointing to his seven claims painted on the tail of his aircraft, MM9066 151-2 of 151ª Squadriglia, 20° *Gruppo*, 51° *Stormo*. Flying from Gela airfield as wingman for Capitano Furio Niclot Doglio, Tarantola would claim five and three shared destroyed over Malta. He would end the war with ten victories, plus one from his service during the Spanish Civil War (*Tony Holmes Collection*)

fell to Australian ace Flt Sgt Jack Yarra of No 185 Sqn during the afternoon attack on Luqa, although the RAF unit in turn lost two Spitfires and their pilots. Ironically, the Macchi pilots claimed five Spitfires badly damaged, but none shot down.

The next big clashes between British and Italian fighters took place on 10 July, and three C.202s were lost during two raids. Capitano Niclot Doglio and Maresciallo Tarantola shared in the destruction of a Spitfire, one of four claimed during the morning raid – Tarantola's fighter was also badly damaged. Niclot Doglio was credited with a second shortly thereafter, with three pilots also sharing a Spitfire between them. None were lost, however. Two more were claimed in the afternoon, when one RAF fighter was indeed shot down. One of two C.202s from 378ª *Squadriglia* downed during the second mission fell to Sgt Beurling, as he subsequently recounted;

'The "Eyetie" went into a steep dive, pulled out and twisted away, rolled and pulled into a climb. Finally, he went into a loop at the end of this climb and I nabbed him just at its top. A two-second burst blew his cockpit apart. The pilot bailed out in a hell of a hurry.'

His victim was Sergente Maggiore Francesco Visentini of 378ª *Squadriglia*, who was rescued by a Z.506B floatplane. A third fighter from the unit was also badly damaged. The *Folgore* units had taken a beating on the 10th, with a number of pilots only avoiding being shot down by performing a series of violent diving manoeuvres in an attempt to shake off pursuing Spitfires. Upon returning to Sicily, a handful of aviators reported encountering the vibration phenomenon caused by compressibility when diving away from, or after, Spitfires. More and more 51° *Stormo* pilots subsequently encountered this problem, which had first affected the fighter of Capitano Carlo Miani. Thinking his C.202 had been badly hit, he bailed out over the Sicilian coast.

Capitano Niclot Doglio claimed another Spitfire shot down and a share in the destruction of a second one on 11 July when seven Macchis clashed with No 249 Sqn during an afternoon raid on Takali. One Spitfire was indeed lost, and a second one crash-landed. For once, no C.202s were shot down.

On the morning of the 13th, ten *Folgores* from 20° *Gruppo* engaged 12 Spitfires during an escort mission for 18 Ju 88s sent to bomb Luqa. Capitano Niclot Doglio was again in the thick of the action, claiming two of the three Spitfires credited to 151ª *Squadriglia*. The unit lost two C.202s and their pilots in return. Actual Spitfire losses amounted to one aircraft from No 126 Sqn, with three more damaged.

The *Regia Aeronautica*'s Malta offensive was now virtually at a standstill, with the bomber campaign having been all but left to the Luftwaffe and the *Folgores* of 51° *Stormo* suffering worsening serviceability due to mounting technical problems. The issues blighting the C.202s were familiar ones –faulty oxygen systems, fragile undercarriage locking mechanisms and tail vibration issues – with the aircraft built under licence by Breda being particularly badly affected.

C.202s returned to Maltese skies from 25 July, with both *gruppi* sending aircraft aloft as escorts for German bombers attacking RAF airfields. *Folgores* and Spitfires clashed again on the morning of the 27th, when 13 C.202s (11 from 20° *Gruppo* and two from 155° *Gruppo*) were assigned as indirect escort for nine Ju 88s. Twenty-two Spitfires from Nos 185, 249 and 126 Sqns were scrambled to intercept the formation, and as they began their attacks on the Ju 88s, the Italian fighter pilots attempted to protect the bombers. No 249 Sqn spotted the Macchis approaching, and Sgt Beurling latched onto a C.202 and shot the fighter down when he hit its engine and radiator with a straight deflection shot. His victim was Sergente Maggiore Faliero Gelli of 378ª *Squadriglia* (who had himself claimed three Malta Spitfires destroyed).

As he had done so many times before, Beurling methodically moved onto his next target and opened fire. 'The poor devil simply blew to pieces in the air', he later explained. His victim was none other than Capitano Furio Niclot Doglio, the leading Italian ace of the Malta campaign. His fighter had been mortally hit, and it crashed into the sea before the pilot could bail out. For the Italians it was a body blow, squadronmate Tenente Ronaldo Scaroni recalling;

'When he died, some of the fighting spirit of the *Regia Aeronautica* died with him. There was a feeling that if Niclot Doglio couldn't survive, none of us could. For the first time we began to doubt that Malta could be taken.'

Capitano Niclot Doglio was subsequently awarded a posthumous *Medaglia d'Oro al Valor Militare*. He was the last C.202 pilot killed in action over Malta during July 1942, and at month-end Generale Silvio Scaroni, commanding general of the *Aeronautica della Sicilia*, ordered all further operations by the *Folgore* to be suspended until serviceability issues had been resolved.

A limited number of missions were flown by C.202s (primarily assigned to 54° *Stormo* on Pantelleria) during August in response to Royal Navy convoys attempting to get urgently needed supplies to Malta. These aircraft rarely encountered the enemy, however.

Following a quiet September, October 1942 would see a renewed effort by both the *Regia Aeronautica* and the Luftwaffe in what would ultimately prove to be the final attempt

This C.202 was also downed by Sgt George Beurling on the same day he claimed Capitano Doglio Niclot's *Folgore*. Sergente Maggiore Faliero Gelli of 378ª *Squadriglia*, 155° *Gruppo*, 51° *Stormo* survived his crash-landing near Victoria, the capital of Gozo, and was pulled from the fighter in an unconscious state after smashing his face on the instrument panel when he hit the ground (*Tony Holmes Collection*)

C.202s from 360ª *Squadriglia*, 155° *Gruppo*, 51° *Stormo* in formation over the Mediterranean in August 1942. Based at Gela from 30 May through to 11 November, 51° *Stormo* would see plenty of action over Malta. Indeed, it was considered to be the most successful Italian fighter unit involved in the campaign, with its pilots claiming more than 150 victories for the loss of 27 C.202s and 16 pilots killed (*Tony Holmes Collection*)

Maresciallo Pasquale Bartolucci of 360ª *Squadriglia*, 155° *Gruppo*, 51° *Stormo* poses in front of his C.202. Bartolucci claimed two Spitfires shot down during the fighting over Malta, and he finished the war with four personal and two shared victories to his name. Note that ten small mice have been added below the unit insignia, which usually featured a black cat catching three green rodents. These additional mice represented victories claimed by 360ª *Squadriglia* over Malta (*Tony Holmes Collection*)

made by the Axis powers to neutralise Malta. The Italians mustered close to 100 C.202s from 51° and 53° *Stormi*, the latter unit having flown 35 *Folgores* from Caselle, near Turin, to Santo Pietro di Caltagirone, on Sicily, in early September.

During the 'October Blitz', which ran from the 11th to the 18th, the pilots of 53° *Stormo*'s 153° *Gruppo* would engage RAF fighters on 14 separate occasions, but they were only able to claim three Spitfires destroyed, five probables and several damaged. As with previous campaigns against Malta, there was excessive overclaiming by both sides. On 12 October, for example, Spitfire pilots were credited with three C.202s destroyed when, in reality, 51° *Stormo* had had three aircraft damaged. Three C.202s were, however, lost to Spitfires the following day, two of them from 153° *Gruppo*.

51° *Stormo* exacted a modicum of revenge for these losses on 14 October when two Spitfires from No 1435 Sqn were downed (three were claimed by *Folgore* pilots), one of these aircraft falling to C.202 ace Maresciallo Tarantola. His aircraft was in turn badly shot up, and he had to bail out near the Sicilian coast.

The 'October Blitz' petered out over the next four days, with the Spitfire pilots having blunted the raids on their airfields by inflicting notable casualties on the Axis bomber units involved, despite the presence of a significant number of escorting fighters. For the rest of the month the *Regia Aeronautica* and the Luftwaffe reverted to fighter sweeps and small-scale *Jabo* fighter-bomber raids using bomb-carrying Re.2001s and Bf 109s, usually escorted by *Folgores*. These missions were more nuisance than effective.

The last C.202 claimed by the RAF over Malta fell to Plt Off Mike Giddings of No 249 Sqn on 24 October, although there was no corresponding loss that day according to Italian records. The last victories credited to *Folgore* pilots during the campaign came 24 hours later

Photographed at San Pietro di Caltagirone in October 1942, this C.202 of 374ª *Squadriglia*, 153° *Gruppo*, 53° *Stormo* managed to return to Sicily despite being shot up by Spitfires over Malta. Note the small RAF roundel between the '6' and the *gruppo* insignia denoting where the fighter had been struck by a 0.303-in. round in combat (*Author's Collection*)

when single Spitfires were claimed by 153° *Gruppo* and 51° *Stormo*. No 126 Sqn ace Sgt Nigel Park was indeed killed in action that day. The final significant raid involving C.202s over Malta occurred on 28 October when six *Jabos* escorted by about 60 C.202s and Bf 109s attacked Luqa airfield. Spitfires from Nos. 126 and 229 Sqns scrambled to engage the enemy aircraft but no interceptions were made.

By the end of October the siege of Malta was all but over.

CHAPTER THREE

FIGHTING OVER NORTH AFRICA

A s noted in the previous chapter, the arrival of C.202s in North Africa was accelerated in the wake of the successful British offensive, codenamed Operation *Crusader*, launched in the Western Desert on 18 November 1941. Although suffering heavy losses, the Eighth Army succeeded in relieving the siege of Tobruk and regaining ground captured by Axis forces during the course of that year.

The *Regia Aeronautica*'s 5ª *Squadra Aerea*, which controlled all aircraft in-theatre, was quickly reinforced with an additional seven fighter *gruppi* in November–December, four of which were equipped with brand new tropicalised C.202ASs – AS stood for *Africa Settentrionale*. These aircraft were fitted with sand filters and featured mottled camouflage. The first *Folgore* units to reach Libya (between 23–25 November) were 9° *Gruppo*'s 96ª and 97ª *Squadriglie*, with 18 C.202s between them, and 17° *Gruppo*'s 71ª *Squadriglia*. All three *squadriglie* were deployed to Martuba.

With the Tomahawks and Hurricanes of the newly formed Desert Air Force (DAF) increasingly dominating the Italian fighter units equipped with C.200s, CR.42s and G.50s in the skies over the Western Desert, the arrival of the C.202s came at a critical moment for 5ª *Squadra Aerea*. With little time to acclimatise to operations, 9° *Gruppo* went into action

Two C.202s from 73ª *Squadriglia*, 9° *Gruppo*, 4° *Stormo* await their next mission from Fuka in early August 1942. MM7823 73-7 was usually flown by ace Tenente Giulio Reiner, who had taken command of 73ª *Squadriglia* the previous month. He would claim seven victories in the space of six months prior to leading his unit from Tripoli to Sicily in January 1943. MM7936 73-10 was shot down by a Spitfire VC from No 92 Sqn on 19 August, with its wounded pilot, Sottotenente Rinaldo Gibellini, bailing out. He later died in captivity (*Tony Holmes Collection*)

Generale d'Armata Ugo Cavallero (centre), Head of the Royal Italian Armed Forces General Staff, chats with Generale di Squadra Aerea Francesco Pricolo (left), the Chief of Staff of the Regia Aeronautica, at Rome-Ciampino airport on 30 October 1941. Both officers were inspecting the brand new C.202s of 1° Stormo's 17° Gruppo, which were en route to Libya from Campoformido. Standing at the extreme right is gruppo CO, Tenente Colonnello Bruno Brambilla (Aeronautica Militare-Fototeca Storica)

These C.202s of 17° Gruppo's 72ª Squadriglia were photographed shortly after 4° Stormo reached Martuba in late November 1941 (Tony Holmes Collection)

on 26 November when ten fighters (five each from 96ª and 97ª Squadriglie) led by gruppo CO, Capitano Antonio Larsimont Pergameni, undertook a sweep between Sidi Rezegh and Gambut.

Nearing Sidi Rezegh, Larsimont Pergameni was the first to sight enemy aircraft below him, with a second group of fighters above them at higher altitude. The Folgores had run into 23 Hurricanes from Nos 229 and 238 Sqns. Using their height advantage, the Macchis, led by Larsimont Pergameni, downed four Hurricanes from No 238 Sqn without loss (two Folgores were badly holed) in an engagement that lasted ten minutes. Upon returning to base, the Italian pilots claimed eight kills and one probable.

Amongst those credited with victories was future 97ª Squadriglia ace Sergente Maggiore Massimo Salvatore, who claimed two kills. His flight engineer, Sergente Maggiore Michele Morelli, later recalled;

'When Massimo landed, we saw that his aircraft's windscreen and canopy was blackened with burned oil, leading us to believe that our Macchi had been hit. As Massimo climbed out of the cockpit, he reassured us that the oil was from an enemy fighter that he had holed at close range – the fluid had leaked all over our '202. Massimo then explained that he had fired at the formation leader rather than at a "tail-end wingman because the latter would have probably been the same rank as me".'

Future aces Tenenti Giovanni Barcaro and Fernando Malvezzi of 96ª Squadriglia and Tenente Emanuele Annoni of 97ª Squadriglia were also credited with single victories.

17° Gruppo experienced its first action on 4 December when 11 C.202s from its three squadriglie flew as escorts (along with C.200s and Bf 109s) for German and Italian Ju 87s attacking Allied targets in the El Adem area. The Folgores clashed with 21 Hurricanes from No 274 Sqn and No 1 Sqn South African Air Force (SAAF). In another example of optimistic claiming, the C.202 pilots were credited with eight victories and one probable when only a single SAAF Hurricane had in fact been downed.

The South African pilots claimed two C.202s destroyed and three probables, and two Folgores were indeed forced down and two damaged.

Two days later, 12 C.202s from 9° Gruppo had just taken off as part of an escort for German Ju 87s targeting British tanks south of El Gubi when disaster struck. Ten minutes into the mission, Sottotenente Barcaro was forced to land when his undercarriage only partially retracted. When Maresciallo Raffaello Novelli moved up to take his place, he collided with Sergente Maggiore Anselmo Andraghetti and both fighters crashed. Although Andraghetti bailed out, seven-victory ace Novelli was killed. Fellow ace Maresciallo Rinaldo Damiani witnessed the accident;

'That day we had to carry out a mission jointly with a German group [I. and/or II./JG 27]. On taking off, Novelli yawed due to the strong transverse wind and lost some minutes in the climb. Shortly thereafter I realised that the undercarriage of the aircraft behind me on the left was not completely retracted. I waved at

A 1° *Stormo* tenente with his C.202. Note the weathering of the propeller, and the exhaust streaking over the wing root (*Archivio Ufficio Storico Stato Maggiore Esercito-Archivio Fotografico*)

the pilot and he turned back. At the same time, while I closed in on Andraghetti after he had replaced Novelli as Larsimont's left wingman, I saw Novelli climbing at full throttle to belatedly take up his position. As he manoeuvred to do so, his rudder struck Andraghetti's wing, causing both fighters to fall away in a spin. I followed them while I was closing in on Larsimont, and I saw Andraghetti bail out (he wore a red flying helmet) and Novelli's fighter hit the ground.'

C.202s from both 9° and 17° *Gruppi* traded blows with DAF fighters on several occasions through to month-end, and although honours were pretty much even with respect to aircraft lost by either side, Axis forces continued to surrender ground to the Eighth Army. When compared to their Allied counterparts, the C.202 force in North Africa was always modest in size – just 18 aircraft were assigned to 9° *Gruppo* and 29 to 17° *Gruppo* for much of 1941. The latter *gruppo*, which was part of 1° *Stormo*, was gradually joined during December by 6° *Gruppo* and its three *squadriglie* (79ª, 81ª and 88ª) at Martuba.

Despite the increased number of C.202s in-theatre, Axis forces were now in full retreat. Unserviceable *Folgores* were duly lost when airfields had to be abandoned, or were attacked by the DAF, and after a hard month of operations, 9° *Gruppo*, now based at Tamet, left Libya for Italy on 29 December. The unit handed its surviving C.202s over to 1° *Stormo*, which would fight on in North Africa until mid-July 1942.

Axis airfields were now being increasingly targeted by raiding parties from the Special Air Service (SAS) and the Long Range Desert Group, and just 24 hours before 9° *Gruppo* left the theatre, Tamet was hit for a second time. 1° *Stormo* suffered a serious blow when nine newly arrived C.202s from 17° *Gruppo* were destroyed by explosive charges. The attackers escaped unscathed into the night.

By early January 1942 Allied armies had advanced halfway across Libya to El Agheila, although their planned conquest of the whole country was thwarted when Generaloberst Erwin Rommel's *Afrika Korps* launched its second offensive of the Desert War on 21 January. All available fighter units were committed to the counter-attack, harrying retreating Allied troops. On 29 January Axis forces had retaken Benghazi, which was occupied by Italian fighter units, including 21 C.202s from 6° *Gruppo* on 5 February – they soon moved on to Martuba, however. At that stage in the conflict, only the two *gruppi* (6° and 17°) of 1° *Stormo* were equipped with C.202s.

By then, the Eighth Army had retired behind the Gazala line, which led north to the coastal fortifications at Tobruk. Undaunted, Rommel continued his chase, directing all aerial forces to soften up the port stronghold. German bombers carried out the bulk of these attacks during daylight hours, relying on C.200s and C.202s to help provide fighter escort.

The only significant action of note in February involving C.202s took place on the 14th when seven *Folgores* from 6° *Gruppo* bounced 18 Kittyhawks from No 3 Sqn Royal Australian Air Force and No 112 Sqn. The C.202s were escorting CR.42s and C.200s at the time, which had been tasked with strafing British vehicles at Bir Hakeim. The Italian pilots involved in this long clash later reported engaging about 20 'Curtiss P-40s, apparently of a new type' – Kittyhawks had started to reach the DAF from late 1941. Once again, overclaiming was rife on both sides, with Kittyhawk pilots being credited with 20 victories and their opponents four (all to C.202 pilots). Not a single Kittyhawk was shot down, while the *Regia Aeronautica* lost three C.200s and two C.202s.

During March, *Folgores* from 1° *Stormo* clashed on several occasions with DAF Kittyhawks during the dogged defence of Martuba airfield, which came under concentrated aerial attack by Allied medium bombers. A total of 21 enemy fighters were credited to *Folgore* pilots during the course of the month, with three C.202s lost in return.

1° *Stormo* also helped directly defend Martuba airfield from Allied artillery when it was shelled on 21 March. Pilots from both *gruppi* flew a series of strafing passes on motor transport supporting the daring Allied attack, with 14 vehicles being destroyed and several damaged. The C.202 of 81ª *Squadriglia's* Sottotenente Alberto Paggi was in turn hit by ground fire and crashed, killing the pilot. Shortly after the failed attack on Martuba, 1° *Stormo* received a further 13 C.202s from Italy, increasing the unit's operational strength to 40 aircraft.

Kittyhawks and C.202s continued to clash in Libyan skies in April, with free sweeps by 1° *Stormo* over the Allied frontline resulting in largescale engagements on the 3rd, 6th and 13th. The Italian pilots involved again heavily overclaimed, with ten victories being credited to them for the loss of two C.202s.

After several weeks of stalemate, the Italo-German offensive to break through the Gazala–Bir Hakeim line recommenced on 26 May. Italian forces had been bolstered for this campaign – known as the Battle of Ain Gazala–Tobruk – with the arrival of 4° *Stormo* from Sicily just 48 hours prior to the start of the offensive. Commencing its third operational tour in North Africa, the unit was posted to Martuba, which now housed more than 100 C.202s; the largest concentration of *Folgores* ever assembled in Libya. Seven of these aircraft were lost (and a further 11 damaged) on the ground in daily Allied bombing raids of the airfield from 25 to 28 May, although 1° *Stormo* pilots also claimed nine 'P-40s' destroyed during a sweep on the 25th – they had in fact tangled with Hurricanes, and only one was shot down.

In a surprise attack to launch the Axis offensive on the morning of the 26th, no fewer than 59 C.202s from both *stormi* strafed the Allied airfield at Gambut. Some 24 Kittyhawks were found neatly parked wing-to-wing on the ground, and these were attacked. Although the Italian pilots claimed to have 'wiped out' the Allied fighters, RAF records show that only a handful of aircraft were damaged.

Both 1° and 4° *Stormi* would be heavily involved in the successful campaign in the Western Desert during the spring and summer of 1942, fighting DAF Kittyhawks, Hurricanes and, increasingly, Spitfires for control of the skies over eastern Libya and western Egypt. *Folgores* also undertook strafing missions in support of Axis troops as they rapidly advanced eastward. During the first two weeks of the spring offensive alone, from 26 May through to the capture of Bir Hakeim on 11 June, C.202 units flew 1093 sorties.

As Allied strongholds from Bir Hakeim to Tobruk fell, so *Folgore* units were ordered to move from Martuba so as to keep pace with the ever changing frontline. 4° *Stormo* was sent to El Adem on 23 June and then on to Sidi el Barrani two days later. Aircraft from both sides were always vulnerable to aerial attack when on the ground at spartan airfields during the fighting in North Africa, and on 26 June 9° *Gruppo* was dealt a serious blow just 24 hours after arriving at Sidi el Barrani.

On 26 June 1942 4° *Stormo* lost the CO of 9° *Gruppo*, *Maggiore* Antonio Larsimont Pergameni, when he was killed in an air raid on Sidi el Barrani airfield (*USSMA*)

At 1500 hrs the airfield was targeted by DAF medium bombers, and an explosion directly in front of the *gruppo* staff tent killed unit CO, Maggiore Antonio Larsimont Pergameni, and two other *Folgore* pilots, as well as a German Flak officer. Tenente Emanuele Annoni recalled the attack, which happened shortly after 9° *Gruppo* pilots had landed following a successful combat with DAF fighters;

'Larsimont, who had been sheltering in a hole at the edge of the airfield, came out to make sure all his pilots had returned safely. The noise of roaring aircraft engines and the movement of taxiing fighters had diverted our attention from a possible enemy air attack. Sure enough, at that very moment, a small formation of bombers approached from the sea and arrived overhead without anyone sounding the alarm. They swept in across the airfield's western side, dropping a line of bombs on both parked aircraft and nearby tents used by *gruppo* and *squadriglie* staff.'

At the end of June 1° *Stormo* was repatriated to Italy, with its surviving *Folgores* being passed on to 4° *Stormo*. In mid-July 23° *Gruppo* returned to North Africa for its second tour in-theatre. With its arrival in Libya, the C.202 force increased to 93 fighters in total, divided between 4° *Stormo* (9° and 10° *Gruppi*), 3° *Stormo* (23° *Gruppo*) and 150° *Gruppo Autonomo* (defending Benghazi).

Having swapped its C.200s for C.202s at Rome-Ciampino in the spring, 23° *Gruppo* had expected to be sent to Sicily until it was decided that the *Folgores* were more urgently needed on the North African front. Consisting of 70ª, 74ª and 75ª *Squadriglie*, 23° *Gruppo*'s experiences in North Africa through to year-end were typical of those units equipped with *Folgores* in-theatre during this period of sustained action.

Flying from Abu Haggag, in Egypt, from 16 July through to 22 October, the *gruppo* initially escorted CR.42s and C.200s on fighter-bomber missions against retreating Allied motor transport. From the end of July,

C.202s had to be flown west to Abu Smeit on a nightly basis so as to escape RAF night bombing raids on Abu Haggag. Routinely engaging various DAF fighters over the next two months, the *gruppo* grappled with worsening serviceability issues through to the end of August due to its C.202s having been rushed to the frontline before sand filters had been installed. These were eventually fitted under operational conditions.

During the Battle of Alam el Halfa, between 30 August and 5 September (the last big Axis offensive of the campaign in North Africa), 23° *Gruppo* achieved a 60 per cent serviceability rate, claiming 18 aircraft for the loss of three C.202s in 175 sorties. By 20 September, the unit had 20 *Folgores* on charge. Subsequent spells of heavy rain left forward airfields all but unusable, and high desert winds in mid-October prevented many missions from being flown. Nightly bombing raids also took a toll, and the *gruppo* was forced to move farther west on the eve of the Second Battle of El Alamein. Serviceability was now down to 40 per cent, with just 12 to 15 aircraft available on a daily basis. It received 12 C.202s from 4° *Stormo* on 30 October.

On 5 November, 23° *Gruppo* was one of the last *Regia Aeronautica* units to pull out of the frontline in Egypt, retreating to Cyrenaica. From here, its pilots help stall the Allied advance across Libya. By 17 January 1943, the *gruppo* had been sent to Castel Benito to help in the ill-fated defence of Tripoli. It then moved to Tunisia shortly thereafter, fighting on until all personnel were evacuated to Sicily at the end of March. The *gruppo* left its few remaining fighters behind for 54° *Stormo*.

ACES HIGH

Being the best Italian fighter in North Africa, the C.202 was the mount of the leading aces of the *Regia Aeronautica* in-theatre. The majority of them served with 4° *Stormo*, seeing combat during Rommel's offensive east and then fighting a rearguard action during the retreat west. Pilots such as Franco Lucchini, Leonardo Ferrulli, Luigi Giannella, Mario Veronesi, Fernando Malvezzi, Giulio Reiner, Emanuele Annoni and Teresio Martinoli claimed the lion's share of their victories between May and early November 1942.

Sergente Maggiore Martinoli, for example, was credited with six P-40s, two Spitfires and a 'P-39' (almost certainly a Kittyhawk) destroyed during this period. Capitano Lucchini, who would end the war as Italy's second-ranking ace, went one better, claiming four P-40s, two Spitfires, two Hurricanes and a Boston, plus more than a dozen shared victories, prior to being badly wounded attacking USAAF B-25s and their escorting P-40s on 24 October – the opening day of the pivotal Second Battle of El Alamein.

Although 18° *Gruppo* only received 12 war-weary C.202s from 4° *Stormo* in October as replacements for 13 C.200s lost to aerial bombing, veteran pilot Tenente Franco Bordoni Bisleri wasted no time in adding to his previous victories in the CR.42. Between 20 October and 7 November, he claimed six P-40s and a Boston shot down, making him the *gruppo*'s leading *Folgore* ace of the campaign. Two of the P-40s were credited to him on 1 November when the four C.202s he was leading fought with

Sergente Maggiore Teresio Martinoli was Italy's ranking ace in World War 2, with 22 and 8 shared confirmed victories. Three victories were claimed in CR.42s, three and one shared in C.205Vs and 16 and seven shared in C.202s. The vast majority of his kills came whilst he was flying with 73ª *Squadriglia*, 9° *Gruppo*, 4° *Stormo* over Malta, in North Africa and in the defence of Sicily. Martinoli lost his life when his P-39 Airacobra crashed near Campo Vesuvio (Naples) on 25 August 1944 whilst he was undergoing conversion training onto the American fighter (*USSMA*)

12 Kittyhawks from No 250 Sqn over Mersa Matruh. The engagement lasted ten minutes, and the ace subsequently recalled;

'I pulled up sharply to dodge the fire of an English pilot, and as I climbed I saw nine more enemy fighters going after my unlucky wingman, Sottotenente Roberto Caetani. I quickly dived back into the fray, and indescribable chaos then ensued. Although we were two against 15, we fared well. Caetani managed to shoot down an aircraft, and I threw two down.'

This action would earn Bordoni Bisleri his third *Medaglia d'Argento al Valor Militare*, with Caetani also being decorated.

Although the C.202 pilots did their best to provide air superiority to increasingly pressed Axis forces on the ground, they were routinely stymied in their efforts by mechanical problems with their aircraft. When Rommel launched his final largescale offensive of the Desert War on 30 August, the *Folgore* had a declared average serviceability rate of just 60 per cent, which compared with the DAF figure of between 73 and 77 per cent for its fighters.

The Western Desert was an operational theatre that tested high performance aircraft like the C.202 to their limits. Sand found its way into everything, and when mixed with engine oil, it produced a ruinous abrasive 'sludge'. Air filters that prevented sand from being sucked into engines when running on the ground were only made available to Italian fighters late on in the campaign, hence the problems that afflicted the C.202. Furthermore, the many different types, and models, of fighter in use with the *Regia Aeronautica* by late 1942 created further maintenance problems, for spare parts were never available in abundance.

The Allied victory at the Second Battle of El Alamein marked the beginning of the end for Axis forces in North Africa. The DAF fielded in excess of 1000 fighters and bombers when the offensive commenced, opposed by 700 German and Italian aircraft. Only 150 of the latter were fighters, however. Unsurprisingly, the *Folgore* force was all but overwhelmed, recording at least 27 aerial combats between 22 and 31 October. Fifteen C.202s were shot down during this nine-day period, with four more destroyed and 46 damaged to varying degrees on the ground. *Folgore* pilots had in turn claimed 39 victories.

Rommel ordered Axis troops to commence a fighting retreat westward into Cyrenaica in early November, and by the 12th the last of his forces had left Egypt. Compounding the *Afrika Korps'* problems, four days earlier, a formidable Anglo-American force had invaded the Vichy French colonies in North Africa as part of Operation *Torch*. Axis forces rapidly fell back on Tripoli, and then Tunisia. This was a sensible move, as Tunisia was the closest point on the African continent from Italian airfields on Sicily, and boasted terrain suited to a 'last ditch' defence with only modest forces.

3° *Stormo* pilots conduct an informal pre-mission briefing at Tauorga, in Tripolitania (now Libya), in late November 1942. The aviators are, from left to right, unknown, 23° *Gruppo* CO and six-victory ace Capitano Giorgio Tugnoli, Sergente Maggiore Zaccaria, Capitano Mario Rigatti and Sergente Maggiore Rolando Garavaldi. The last pilot subsequently joined the pro-German AR following the Armistice, and he was killed in action when his C.205V from 1° *Gruppo Caccia* was shot down by a P-47 from the 325th FG on 13 May 1944 (*Archivio Ufficio Storico Stato Maggiore Esercito-Archivio Fotografico*)

Groundcrew from 23° *Gruppo* help 70ª *Squadriglia* CO and 11-victory ace Capitano Claudio Solaro with his parachute harness at Medenine airfield, in Tunisia, in late January 1943. Behind them is Solaro's tropicalised C.202, which has had its engine started up in preparation for take-off (*Archivio Ufficio Storico Stato Maggiore Esercito-Archivio Fotografico*)

The *Regia Aeronautica* reacted quickly to the invasion, with 24 *Folgores* from 153° *Gruppo* being sent from Palermo, on Sicily, to Decimomannu, on Sardinia, on 7 November. C.202-equipped 17° *Gruppo*, which was already at Decimomannu, and 20° *Gruppo* at nearby Monserrato were also committed to operations immediately post-*Torch* – between them, they could field 65 C.202s. On 11 November, 21 *Folgores* from 155° *Gruppo* flew from Gela to El Aouina airfield in Tunisia. The unit would be committed to operations immediately upon its arrival in-theatre, flying sweeps for Axis bombers targeting Allied vessels in the Algerian ports of Bone and Bougie.

Meanwhile, in Libya, 5ª *Squadra Aerea*'s 2°, 3° and 4° *Stormi* had 66 C.202s between them, based at Martuba, Bu Amud and Benghazi K3. Now fighting the DAF and the USAAF's Ninth Air Force on two fronts, the *Folgore* units began a steady retreat eastward from Libya into Tunisia, while the *gruppi* on Sardinia tried to keep Allied forces at bay in the west.

C.202 units suffered as many losses on the ground as in the air during the final six months of combat in North Africa. For example, on 18 January, Castel Benito, in Libya, was bombed twice by USAAF B-17s, resulting in the destruction of seven C.202s from 3° *Stormo*. Two days later, the unit's 18° *Gruppo* (which had lost five of its *Folgores* in the raid) pulled back to Tunisia, as did 23° *Gruppo*. These were the last flying units of the *Regia Aeronautica* to leave the country. Airfields in Tunisia were no safer, with 18° *Gruppo* losing three more C.202s in an attack on Medenine on 24 January.

Although a number of *Folgore* units had been pulled out of Tunisia by the end of February, a full strength 16° *Gruppo* transferred 30 C.202s from Medenine to Gabes on the 26th. As well as escorting German aircraft attacking Allied positions in southeastern Tunisia, its pilots frequently carried out strafing missions of their own. The *gruppo* also experienced many dogfights in the final weeks of the campaign. For example, on 7 March, the unit was credited with an astounding ten victories (eight Spitfires, a P-38 and a P-40) during an attack on the Neffatia landing ground and overhead Medenine. Two *Folgores* were lost in return. According to Allied records no Spitfires were destroyed on that date.

The partially stripped 'carcass' of C.202 79-10 of 6° *Gruppo*'s 79ª *Squadriglia* at Sfax, in Tunisia, in February 1943. Although the aircraft is missing its wings and various other panels, the fuselage appears to be undamaged (*Tony Holmes Collection*)

Overclaiming was also prevalent amongst the Sardinian units, with 17° *Gruppo* having been credited with two Beaufighters and five Spitfires destroyed on 15 December whilst providing escort for convoys sailing to and from Tunisian ports. Again, no aircraft of either type was lost. (*text continues on page 47*)

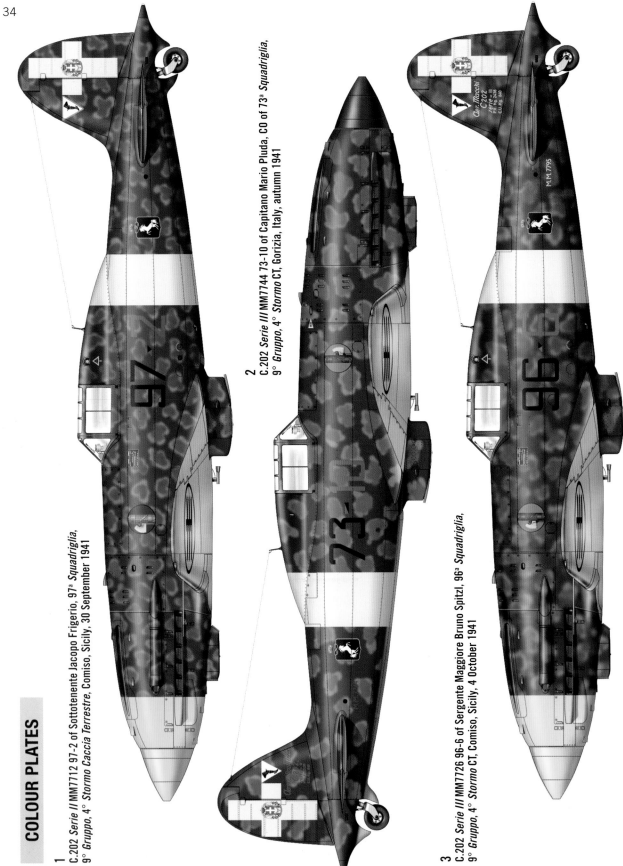

COLOUR PLATES

1
C.202 *Serie II* MM7712 97-2 of Sottotenente Iacopo Frigerio, 97ª *Squadriglia*,
9° *Gruppo*, 4° *Stormo Caccia Terrestre*, Comiso, Sicily, 30 September 1941

2
C.202 *Serie III* MM7744 73-10 of Capitano Mario Pluda, CO of 73ª *Squadriglia*,
9° *Gruppo*, 4° *Stormo CT*, Gorizia, Italy, autumn 1941

3
C.202 *Serie III* MM7726 96-6 of Sergente Maggiore Bruno Spitzl, 96ª *Squadriglia*,
9° *Gruppo*, 4° *Stormo CT*, Comiso, Sicily, 4 October 1941

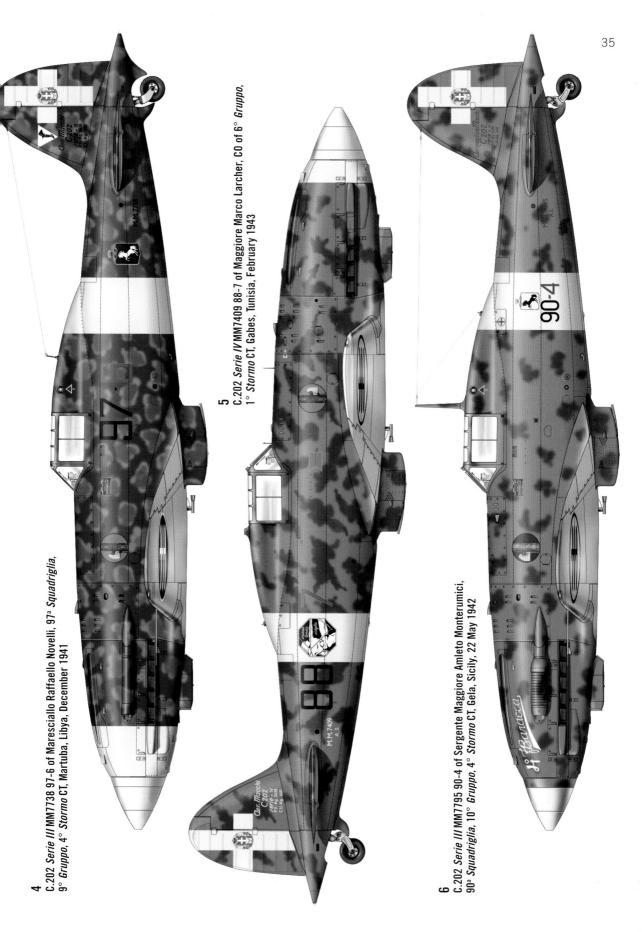

35

35

35

4
C.202 *Serie III* MM7738 97-6 of Maresciallo Raffaello Novelli, 97ª *Squadriglia*,
9° *Gruppo*, 4° *Stormo* CT, Martuba, Libya, December 1941

5
C.202 *Serie IV* MM7409 88-7 of Maggiore Marco Larcher, CO of 6° *Gruppo*,
1° *Stormo* CT, Gabes, Tunisia, February 1943

6
C.202 *Serie III* MM7795 90-4 of Sergente Maggiore Amleto Monterumici,
90ª *Squadriglia*, 10° *Gruppo*, 4° *Stormo* CT, Gela, Sicily, 22 May 1942

35

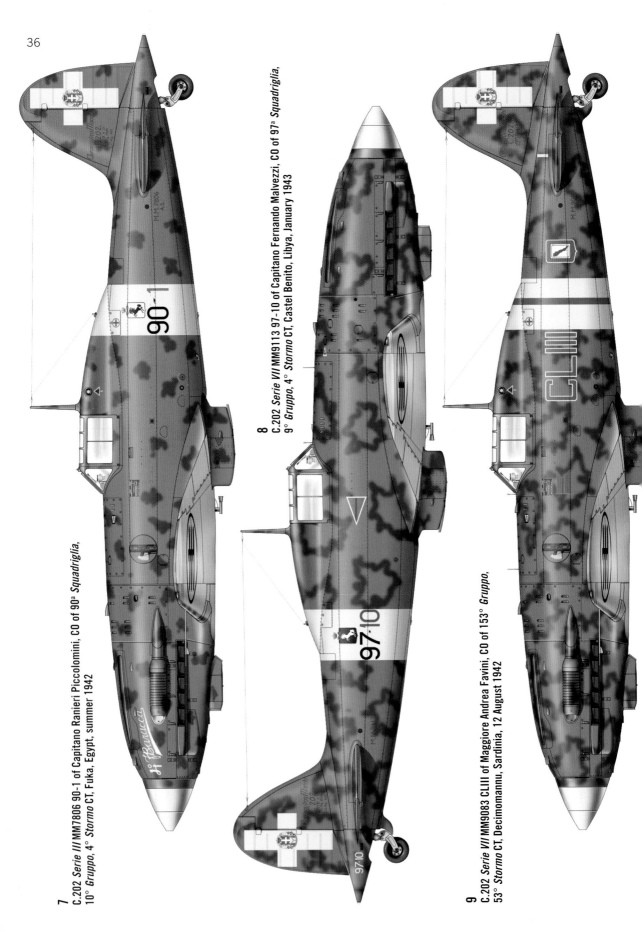

7
C.202 *Serie III* MM7806 90-1 of Capitano Ranieri Piccolomini, CO of 90ª *Squadriglia,*
10° *Gruppo,* 4° *Stormo CT,* Fuka, Egypt, summer 1942

8
C.202 *Serie VII* MM9113 97-10 of Capitano Fernando Malvezzi, CO of 97ª *Squadriglia,*
9° *Gruppo,* 4° *Stormo CT,* Castel Benito, Libya, January 1943

9
C.202 *Serie VII* MM9083 CLIII of Maggiore Andrea Favini, CO of 153° *Gruppo,*
53° *Stormo CT,* Decimomannu, Sardinia, 12 August 1942

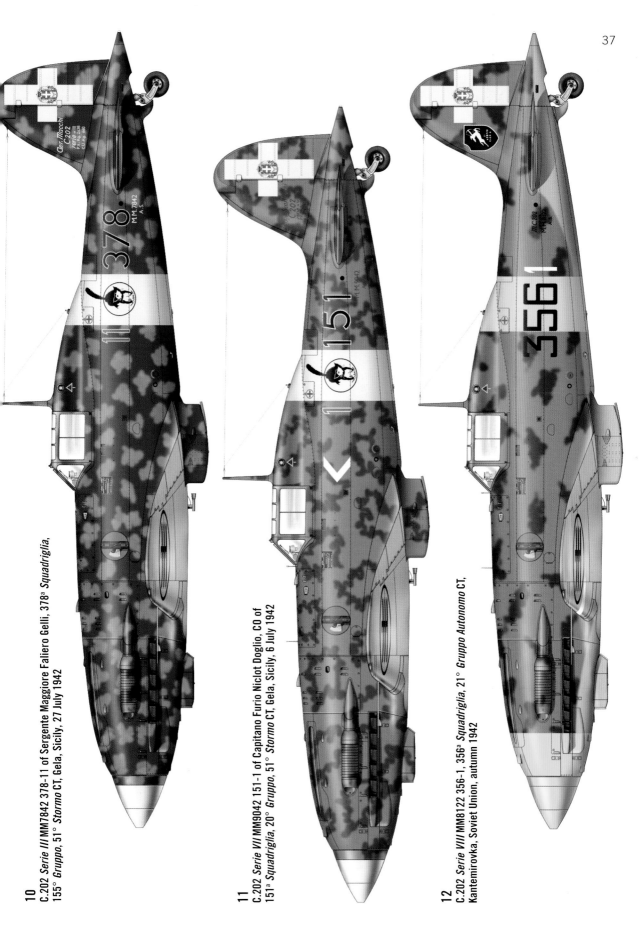

10
C.202 *Serie III* MM7842 378-11 of Sergente Maggiore Faliero Gelli, 378ª *Squadriglia*,
155° *Gruppo*, 51° *Stormo* CT, Gela, Sicily, 27 July 1942

11
C.202 *Serie VII* MM9042 151-1 of Capitano Furio Niclot Doglio, CO of
151ª *Squadriglia*, 20° *Gruppo*, 51° *Stormo* CT, Gela, Sicily, 6 July 1942

12
C.202 *Serie VIII* MM8122 356-1, 356ª *Squadriglia*, 21° *Gruppo Autonomo* CT,
Kantemirovka, Soviet Union, autumn 1942

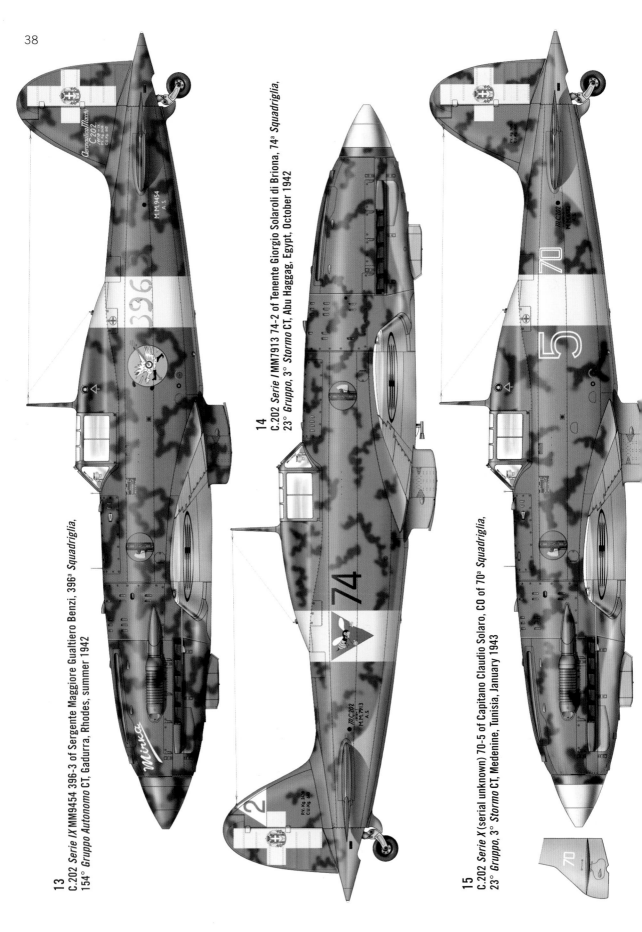

13
C.202 *Serie IX* MM9454 396-3 of Sergente Maggiore Gualtiero Benzi, 396ª *Squadriglia*,
154° *Gruppo Autonomo CT*, Gadurra, Rhodes, summer 1942

14
C.202 *Serie I* MM7913 74-2 of Tenente Giorgio Solaroli di Briona, 74ª *Squadriglia*,
23° *Gruppo*, 3° *Stormo CT*, Abu Haggag, Egypt, October 1942

15
C.202 *Serie X* (serial unknown) 70-5 of Capitano Claudio Solaro, CO of 70ª *Squadriglia*,
23° *Gruppo*, 3° *Stormo CT*, Medenine, Tunisia, January 1943

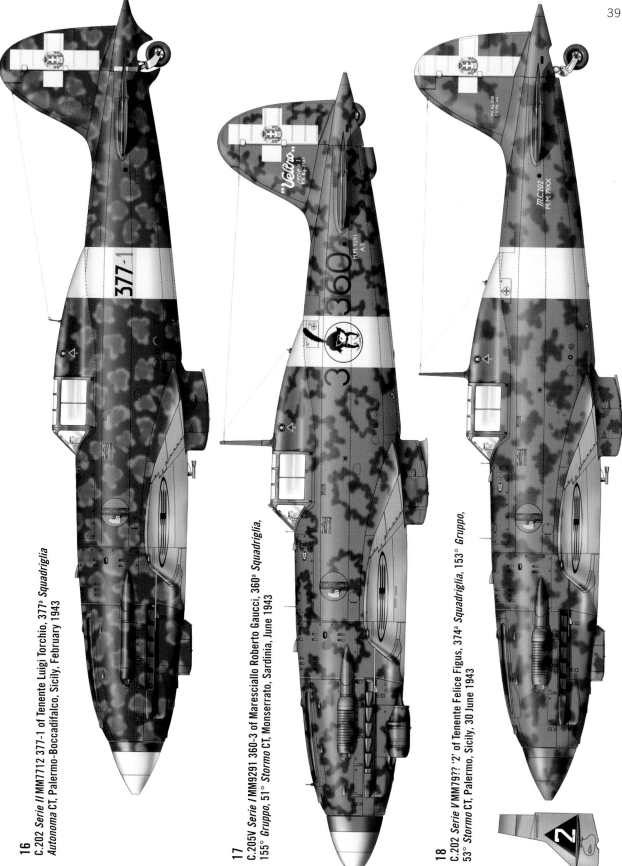

16
C.202 *Serie II* MM7712 377-1 of Tenente Luigi Torchio, 377ª *Squadriglia Autonoma* CT, Palermo-Boccadifalco, Sicily, February 1943

17
C.205V *Serie I* MM9291 360-3 of Maresciallo Roberto Gaucci, 360ª *Squadriglia*, 155° *Gruppo*, 51° *Stormo* CT, Monserrato, Sardinia, June 1943

18
C.202 *Serie V* MM797? '2' of Tenente Felice Figus, 374ª *Squadriglia*, 153° *Gruppo*, 53° *Stormo* CT, Palermo, Sicily, 30 June 1943

40

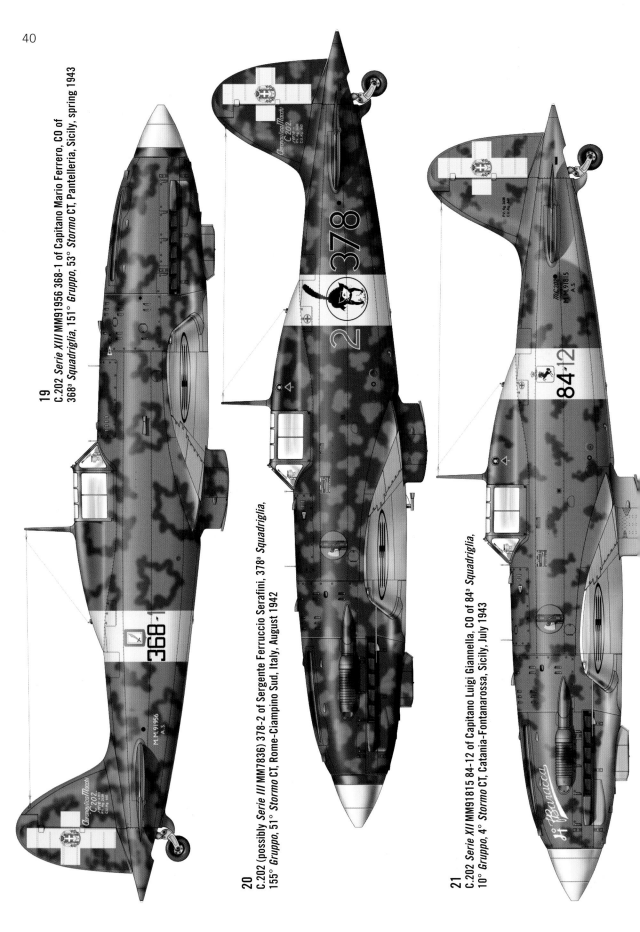

19
C.202 *Serie XII* MM91956 368-1 of Capitano Mario Ferrero, CO of
368ª *Squadriglia*, 151° *Gruppo*, 53° *Stormo* CT, Pantelleria, Sicily, spring 1943

20
C.202 (possibly *Serie III* MM7835) 378-2 of Sergente Ferruccio Serafini, 378ª *Squadriglia*,
155° *Gruppo*, 51° *Stormo* CT, Rome-Ciampino Sud, Italy, August 1942

21
C.202 *Serie XII* MM91815 84-12 of Capitano Luigi Giannella, CO of 84ª *Squadriglia*,
10° *Gruppo*, 4° *Stormo* CT, Catania-Fontanarossa, Sicily, July 1943

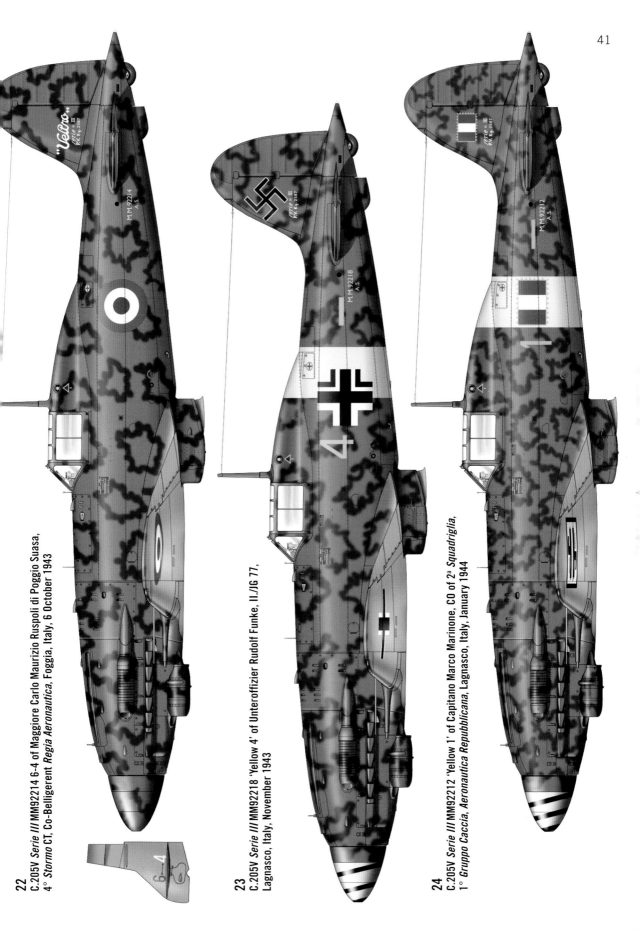

22
C.205V *Serie III* MM92214 6-4 of Maggiore Carlo Maurizio Ruspoli di Poggio Suasa,
4° *Stormo* CT, Co-Belligerent *Regia Aeronautica*, Foggia, Italy, 6 October 1943

23
C.205V *Serie III* MM92218 'Yellow 4' of Unteroffizier Rudolf Funke, II./JG 77,
Lagnasco, Italy, November 1943

24
C.205V *Serie III* MM92212 'Yellow 1' of Capitano Marco Marinone, CO of 2ª *Squadriglia*,
1° *Gruppo Caccia, Aeronautica Repubblicana,* Lagnasco, Italy, January 1944

25
C.205V *Serie III* MM92277 6-2 of Sottotenente Remo Lugari, 2ª *Squadriglia*,
1° *Gruppo Caccia, Aeronautica Repubblicana*, Campoformido, Italy, February 1944

26
C.205V *Serie III* MM92302 23-1 of Sergente Maggiore Luigi Gorrini, 1ª *Squadriglia*,
1° *Gruppo Caccia, Aeronautica Repubblicana*, Campoformido, Italy, spring 1944

27
C.205V *Serie III* MM92276 15-2 of Sottotenente Aurelio Morandi, 2ª *Squadriglia*,
1° *Gruppo Caccia, Aeronautica Repubblicana*, Reggio Emilia, Italy, June 1944

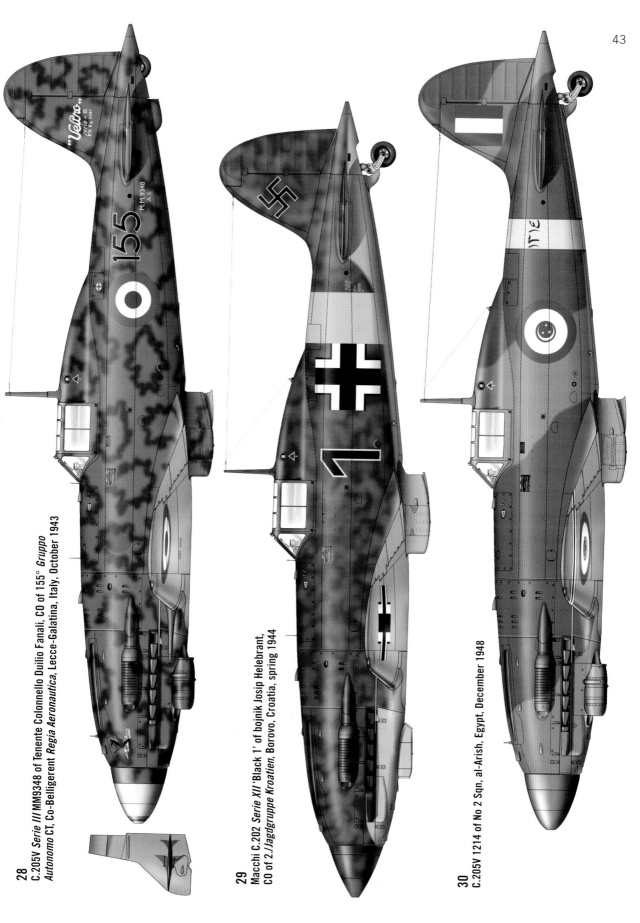

43

28
C.205V *Serie III* MM9348 of Tenente Colonnello Duilio Fanali, CO of 155° *Gruppo Autonomo CT, Co-Belligerent Regia Aeronautica*, Lecce-Galatina, Italy, October 1943

29
Macchi C.202 *Serie XII* 'Black 1' of bojnik Josip Helebrant,
CO of 2./*Jagdgruppe Kroatien*, Borovo, Croatia, spring 1944

30
C.205V 1214 of No 2 Sqn, al-Arish, Egypt, December 1948

UNIT BADGES

1
1° Stormo

2
3° Gruppo

3
3° Stormo

4
4° Stormo

5
5° Stormo

6
8° Gruppo

7
9° Gruppo

8
10° Gruppo

9
21° Gruppo Autonomo

10
22° Gruppo

11
24° Gruppo Autonomo

12
51° Stormo

46

13
150° Gruppo Autonomo

14
151° Gruppo

15
153° Gruppo

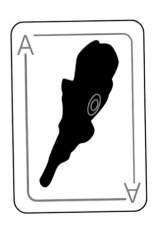

16
1ª Squadriglia, 1° Gruppo Caccia

17
2ª Squadriglia, 1° Gruppo Caccia

18
Tenente Colonnello Duilio Fanali's
personal insignia

A pilot climbs into the cockpit of his idling C.202 at Gabes, in Tunisia, in March 1943. This aircraft is almost certainly from 6° *Gruppo*'s 79ª *Squadriglia*, which was withdrawn to Italy at the end of the month to commence its conversion onto the C.205V (*Tony Holmes Collection*)

Like their counterparts fighting in western Tunisia, Sardinia-based C.202 units also found it tough going as they attempted to provide fighter cover for transport aircraft trying to fly fuel and supplies in to besieged forces in North Africa. 155° *Gruppo*, which had been sent to Tunisia, only remained in-theatre a matter of weeks before it returned to Italy. 18° *Gruppo* followed in early April, having seen its strength reduced from 29 C.202s in early February to just a handful of fighters. It had also moved five times in seven weeks.

Amongst the 18° *Gruppo* pilots that fought virtually to the end of the campaign was Tenente Guglielmo Specker, who was acting CO of 83ª *Squadriglia*. Post-war, he provided the following insight into aspects of the fighting over Tunisia;

'The *Regia Aeronautica* generally employed as its basic formation the column of twos, with each pair stepped slightly higher than the next, and with each section leader having an aircraft on his right wing. The formation flew quite close together until they reached their objective, where they would spread out or maintain formation according to the demands of the mission to be accomplished. The pair was instructed never to separate in order to maintain mutual support and protection at all times.

'The [Tunisian] campaign was difficult due to a reduced number of pilots, technicians and aircraft. We had extreme problems in respect to the supply of spare parts, which meant we struggled with aircraft repairs.

'As far as the enemy fighters were concerned, I remember the most dangerous as being the Spitfire and the Lightning, as both were better armed and more manoeuvrable than the C.202. Less significance was attached to the Curtiss [P-40] and the Hurricane, as they were slower.

'If it is possible to live on love alone, I should say that the *Regia Aeronautica* came pretty close to succeeding from November 1942 to April 1943. With but few pilots and machines, and with both a little more tired each day, they always remained lively and ready to fight. Discouragement was never allowed to take over even in the worst period of the long retreat, and they responded to every call with spirit and pride.'

By the end of March the whole of Libya was in Allied hands. The advance in Tunisia was underway and Eighth Army units would soon link up with elements of the US Army's

C.202s from 23° *Gruppo*'s 74ª *Squadriglia* sit in the open at El Hamma, in Tunisia, in February 1943. 3° *Stormo*'s 18° and 23° *Gruppi* had 19 serviceable C.202s at this airfield on 15 February when the unit became part of 5ª *Squadra*'s newly formed *Settore Sud* (Southern Sector). Four of 23° *Gruppo*'s *Folgores* were destroyed and two damaged when El Hamma was attacked by Allied medium bombers on 27 February (*Tony Holmes Collection*)

II Corps advancing from western Tunisia. The Axis forces that remained would now be pushed into the northeast corner of the country.

The only C.202-equipped units in North Africa by May were 7° and 16° *Gruppi* of 54° *Stormo* based at Soliman and nearby Korba, respectively, on the northeastern coast of Tunisia. The final aerial action between Allied fighters and the *stormo* took place on the 6th, when 14 *Folgores* from 7° *Gruppo* on patrol near Cap Bon engaged 'P-40s'

Capitano Giuliano Giacomelli, CO of 6° *Gruppo*'s 81ª *Squadriglia*, eases himself into the cockpit of C.202 81-10 at El Achichina, in Tunisia, in late February 1943 (*Tony Holmes Collection*)

– they were actually USAAF Spitfires from the 31st FG. Two kills were claimed by the Italian pilots, one of whom was future ten-victory ace Capitano Adriano Visconti. No Spitfires were lost, however. A C.202 was shot down (and Capitano Sergio Maurer killed) and a second example, flown by *Stormo* CO Tenente Colonnello Giovanni Zappetta, was forced to crash land.

At dawn on 8 May all 19 serviceable C.202s from 7° *Gruppo* left Soliman for Korba, where, later that day, they were repeatedly strafed by DAF Spitfires. Shortly thereafter, 54° *Stormo* was given permission to leave for Castelvetrano. Just before dawn on the 9th, 12 C.202s departed for Sicily, with four of the aircraft carrying 'passengers' in order to save them from captivity. The attempt to extricate the *stormo*'s remaining pilots failed when the S.82 transport aircraft flown in under the cover of darkness to pick them up could not take off again due to the damage it had suffered in the devastating attack on Korba.

In 13 May 1943, Generale Giovanni Messe surrendered 248,000 Axis troops in Tunisia to Allied forces. Amongst this number were 37 *Folgore* pilots from 54° *Stormo*. Two weeks later, the unit was disbanded.

When the fighting in Tunisia ended in mid-May 1943, a number of wrecked C.202s were found lined up in a dump near Al Aouina airfield. Six months later, these aircraft were picked over for parts by the Co-Belligerent *Regia Aeronautica* in order to keep its remaining *Folgores* airworthy (*Tony Holmes Collection*)

CHAPTER FOUR

OTHER THEATRES

Between 11 and 15 August 1942, 21 C.202s of 153° *Gruppo* were deployed to Decimomannu airfield, and from here they participated in the attacks on the Malta-bound 'Pedestal' convoy. In the air battle fought over the vessels on 12 August, *gruppo* pilots claimed to have shot down five Hurricanes, with a sixth as a probable, for no losses in return (*Author's Collection*)

MEDITERRANEAN

As briefly noted in chapter two, Sicily- and Pantelleria-based *Folgores* played a minor role in Axis operations aimed at enforcing the siege of Malta during the summer of 1942. German and Italian dive- and torpedo-bombers were heavily tasked with attacking Allied merchantmen, and their naval escorts, as they ran the gauntlet in the central Mediterranean in an attempt to get much needed supplies from Gibraltar to Egypt.

Due to its modest range, the C.202 was not ideally suited to providing escort for bombers targeting such vessels. This in turn meant that there were only a handful of encounters between *Folgores* and Allied aircraft. The first such engagement reportedly took place on 15 June during the Battle of Pantelleria, when Axis aircraft were attempting to sink vessels from the 'Harpoon' convoy. That day, Capitano Adriano Visconti of 7° *Gruppo*'s 76ª *Squadriglia* was sortied from Pantelleria in a camera-equipped C.202 with orders to photograph the naval action taking place nearby between Italian and British warships.

Macchi fighters equipped with photo-planimetric cameras had assumed the photo-reconnaissance role from slower, more vulnerable S.79s and Z.1007s on Sicily and Pantelleria during 1941. 7° *Gruppo* had initially used a small number of locally modified C.200s for such missions over Malta, and in early 1942 these were replaced by C.202s.

During the course of the 15 June mission, Visconti reported encountering a formation of 'Blenheims', which he attacked. He subsequently claimed to have shot one of them down in flames (for his first victory) and damaged a second. There were no Blenheims anywhere near the convoy, so it seems likely Visconti encountered either Beauforts or Beaufighters tasked with providing cover for the 'Harpoon' convoy, or a photo-reconnaissance Baltimore. Crews from all three twin-engined types stated that they were engaged by Axis aircraft, and Beauforts and Beaufighters were indeed lost that day to German fighters.

Visconti's C.202 was not the only *Folgore* in the skies off Pantelleria on the 15th, for 25 fighters from Chinisia-based 155° *Gruppo* had departed Sicily shortly before noon as escorts for Ju 87s

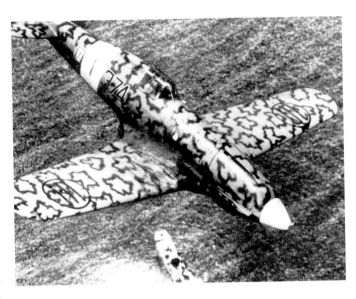

C.202 374-1, flown by 374ª *Squadriglia*'s commanding officer, Capitano Natale Veronesi, makes a pass over a sinking merchantman during the 'Pedestal' battles of August 1942 (*Author's Collection*)

from 102° *Gruppo* that were targeting the 'Harpoon' convoy. The vessels were in turn protected by three flights of Spitfires from No 601 Sqn. In the ensuing engagement, C.202 pilots claimed four Spitfires destroyed and one probable without loss. Among the claimants was 155° *Gruppo* CO Maggiore Duilio Fanali, who was credited with two individual and no fewer than 33 shared victories in 1942 alone. No 601 Sqn lost two Spitfires (one to fuel exhaustion) and had a third fighter slightly damaged.

C.202s next saw action over Allied vessels when the 'Pedestal' convoy headed for Malta in mid-August. The task of protecting the 14 merchantmen that made up the convoy would generate the largest naval/air operation yet attempted by the Royal Navy, as a significant Axis force was ranged against the vessels. No fewer than four warships (including the carrier HMS *Eagle*) and nine merchantmen would be sunk during attacks on the 'Pedestal' convoy, with *Folgores* escorting bombers on 12, 13 and 14 August.

On the morning of the 12th, 14 C.202s from 153° *Gruppo* – led by unit CO Maggiore Andrea Favini – took off from Decimomannu as escorts for S.79 and S.84 torpedo-bombers. South of Sardinia, the Italian aircraft were intercepted by carrier-based Martlets and Sea Hurricanes. Favini's men subsequently claimed five victories and one probable without loss. A single Sea Hurricane was shot down and a second one severely damaged.

At 1725 hrs that same day, 28 *Folgores* from 51° *Stormo*'s 20° and 155° *Gruppi*, led by Tenente Colonnello Aldo Remondino, sortied from Pantelleria as escorts for 13 Stukas from 102° *Gruppo* and 14 S.79s from 132° *Gruppo*. Just prior to their departure, 14 more C.202s from 153° *Gruppo* had also taken off from Sardinia as escorts for eight S.79s. It would appear that only the 51° *Stormo* aircraft encountered the enemy, with seven kills (against fighters identified as Fulmars, Hurricanes and Martlets) being credited to pilots from the unit – one of whom was Maggiore Fanali. A solitary Fulmar was shot down and a second example badly damaged. Although Royal Navy pilots in turn claimed two C.202s destroyed, none were lost.

The following morning, ten *Folgores* from 51° *Stormo* escorted eight Ju 87s from 102° *Gruppo* in an unsuccessful attack on the damaged tanker *Ohio,* clashing with the ship's Spitfire escort – the surviving vessels from the 'Pedestal' convoy were now in range of Malta's fighter force. Maggiore Duilio Fanali duly claimed a Spitfire destroyed, and an aircraft from No 126 Sqn was indeed shot down. Tenente Adriano Visconti was also in action that morning, and he claimed two Spitfires destroyed during the course of another lone photo-reconnaissance mission from Pantelleria.

At 0950 hrs on 14 August 23 *Folgores* from 51° *Stormo,* again led by Tenente Colonnello Remondino, departed Gela as escorts for five Ju 87s from 102° *Gruppo.* Their target was the seemingly unsinkable *Ohio,* which was being escorted by Spitfires from Nos 229 and 1435 Sqns as it limped towards Malta. Whilst protecting the dive-bombers, the C.202 flown by 20° *Gruppo* CO Capitano Egeo Pittoni was shot down by future ace Flt Sgt Ian MacLennan of No 1435 Sqn. His combat report read as follows;

'Fired from 150 yards down to 25 yards. Saw many strikes all along the top of the aircraft. White smoke started pouring out; he turned very slowly to the left, nose slightly up. I closed in to 15 ft or less, firing all over the cockpit, and pieces flew off again. His nose dropped and he kept turning slowly to the left, going down, trailing thick white smoke. I claim this aircraft as destroyed as I think the pilot was dead.'

In fact Pittoni was subsequently rescued by a Luftwaffe Do 24T flying boat escorted by six C.202s from 51° *Stormo.*

No *Folgores* were involved in subsequent actions against Allied convoys in the central Mediterranean.

RECONNAISSANCE MACCHIS

The conversion of *Folgore* fighters into dedicated photo-reconnaissance C.202RFs involved the replacement of the aircraft's near-useless radio unit in the fuselage behind the pilot's seat with a vertical AGR 90 photo-planimetric camera. Some aircraft were also fitted with Kodak 30 cm cameras. The fighters retained full armament. Only a small number of C.202s received cameras, including MM7711 of 378ª *Squadriglia* (155° *Gruppo,* 51° *Stormo*), MM7712 of 377ª *Squadriglia Autonoma* (which was often flown by five-victory ace Tenente Luigi Torchio) and MM7727 of 73ª *Squadriglia* (9° *Gruppo,* 4° *Stormo*).

Aside from the C.202RFs, a small number of *Folgores* were also modified for 'flying propaganda' purposes. The latter were equipped with a single AVIA 35 mm cine camera in the leading edge of both wing. At least seven aircraft (MM7844, 9405, 9406, 9115, 9116, 9425 and 9426) were fitted with cameras and issued to frontline units in 1942. Dubbed 'movie Macchis', they were tasked with filming actual air combat against Allied aircraft. The resulting film footage was then spliced into propaganda newsreels shown to the Italian public.

A total of 12 C.205Vs were also modified into photo-reconnaissance aircraft in May–June 1943. As with the C.202, the *Veltro's* German-built Reihenbilder RB50/30 Zeiss FK 30 photo-planimetric camera was installed in the fuselage immediately behind the cockpit in place of the radio unit, and associated mast, and the aft 80-litre fuel tank. The camera took its photographs through a door-covered opening (which the pilot could open and close from the cockpit) in the underside of the fuselage. The aircraft were modified at the *Regia Aeronautica*'s *Centro Sperimentale* (experimental centre) at Guidonia, near Rome, where the *Veltros* were also fitted with underwing racks for two extra 100- or 150-litre fuel tanks so as to improve the aircrafts' range.

All 12 photo-reconnaissance C.205Vs were initially issued to Guidonia-based 310ª *Squadriglia Caccia Aerofotografica* (Air Photographic Fighter Flight), which had been formed on 30 June 1943 under the leadership of ace Capitano Adriano Visconti. One or two examples were subsequently sent to 4° and 51° *Stormi* (on Sicily and Sardinia, respectively) in order for them to undertake reconnaissance missions over Malta.

Although of indifferent quality, this photograph is worthy of publication by dint of the fact that its subject is a rare 'movie Macchi' – one of only a handful flown by the *Regia Aeronautica*. These C.202s were equipped with a single AVIA 35 mm cine camera in the leading edge of both wings and their pilots tasked with filming actual air combat against Allied aircraft. The tell-tale signs that this fighter boasted cine cameras are the two bumps on the wing leading edges – these housed the camera lenses (*Archivio Ufficio Storico Stato Maggiore Esercito-Archivio Fotografico*)

Engineers at Guidonia also installed cine cameras into eight *Veltros* for propaganda purposes, fitting AVIA or 'Guidon-cine' 35 mm cameras into the wing leading edges as per the C.202 modification. When the cameras were not carried, their housings were plated-over. Again, these aircraft shot actual combat footage for propaganda newsreels.

Whilst flying photo-reconnaissance C.205Vs, 310ª *Squadriglia* was involved in the air defence of Rome – Capitano Visconti scrambled on four occasions (21 and 23 July and 12 and 18 August) but failed to spot the enemy. Squadronmates, and fellow aces, Tenente Giuseppe Robetto and Sergente Domenico Laiolo clashed with P-38s whilst flying modified *Veltros*, sharing one Lightning destroyed between them and suffering modest damage in return.

310ª *Squadriglia* also received several long-range photo-reconnaissance C.205Vs that could carry two 180-litre fuel tanks and were armed with single MG 151 20 mm cannon in each wing. With the fitment of the large external tanks, these *Veltros* had their range extended to 670 miles. Once training on the aircraft was completed, a section of C.205Vs from 310ª *Squadriglia* was deployed to Decimomannu to undertake photo-reconnaissance sorties over Malta, Tunisia, Algeria and the Sicilian Channel. Led by Capitano Visconti, the section's remaining pilots (Tenente Giovanni Sajeva and Sergenti Domenico Laiolo and Maggiore Carlo Magnaghi) also routinely flew cine camera-equipped *Veltros* to supplement the still photographs that were being taken.

When the Armistice put an end to the three-month existence of 310ª *Squadriglia*, Capitano Visconti refused to capitulate. Instead, he flew his *Veltro*, and three of his men, back to the Italian mainland to fight on with the AR.

EASTERN FRONT

Although the *Regia Aeronautica* had had a modest fighter presence on the Eastern Front since August 1941 in the form of C.200-equipped

C.200s and C.202s of 21° *Gruppo Autonomo* lined up on Kantemirovka airfield, on the Eastern Front, in the late summer of 1942. The noses of the Macchi fighters feature the yellow recognition markings that were applied to all Axis aircraft in this theatre. Just 14 C.202s saw combat with 21° *Gruppo* in the USSR (*Author's Collection*)

22° *Gruppo, Folgores* were not committed to this theatre until September 1942 when just 12 (followed by two photo-reconnaissance variants) were assigned to 21° *Gruppo Autonomo* (led by ace Maggiore Ettore Foschini) at Voroshilovgrad airfield. This unit had replaced an exhausted 22° *Gruppo* four months earlier. Once in the USSR, the C.202s were divided among the *gruppo's* four *squadriglie* (356ª, 361ª, 382ª and 386ª).

The *Folgores* were involved in Axis efforts to stem a Soviet counterattack along the east Don river from October, with 21° *Gruppo*, operating from Kantemirovka airfield, sending up mixed formations of C.200s and C.202s to undertake ground attack missions in appalling winter weather. One such sortie on 11 December saw seven C.200s and C.202s from 361ª *Squadriglia* strafing advancing Red Army troops in the Bychek sector, with the Italian fighters being engaged by fierce anti-aircraft fire. The *Folgore* flown by Tenente Gino Lionello was duly hit and he was forced to bail out.

The following day, the *squadriglia* was bounced in the same area by Soviet fighters (probably Yak-7Bs) of 127th IAP, and future 11-kill ace Starshij Leytenant Alexander Petrovic Savchenko shot down the C.200 of Tenente Walter Benedetti. According to 127th IAP's combat report, its pilots had been in action with a group of fighters consisting of three C.200s and one 'Me 109' (clearly a C.202) in the sector between Dubovoj and Dmitrevka.

When the Italian 8th Army's resistance along the Don collapsed under the weight of the Soviet attack, 21° *Gruppo* was forced to fight a rearguard action in an attempt to stall the Red Army advance. The C.202s were tasked with escorting Italian BR.20M and Ca.311 bombers, Z.1007bis reconnaissance aircraft and Ju 52/3ms flying supplies in the direction of Stalingrad.

The 6th Soviet Army's 17th Armoured Corps seized Kantemirovka airfield on 19 December, forcing 21° *Gruppo* to retreat westward. Lacking fuel, parts and munitions, the group flew its final operational mission in-theatre on 17 January 1943 when a mixed formation of 25 C.200s and C.202s targeted a large motorised convoy from the 18th Armoured Corps near Voloshino hamlet in the Millerovo sector. The following day, 21° *Gruppo* was forced to abandon Voroshilovgrad for Stalino. It moved again on 13 February, this time to Odessa airport.

On 27 March, 382ª *Squadriglia* pilot Tenente Pasquale Castellaneta was killed when his C.202 crashed during a training flight – he was the last Italian airman to perish on the Eastern Front.

Rugged up against the biting cold, a pilot from 21° *Gruppo's* 356ª *Squadriglia* poses in front of C.202 *Serie VIII* MM8122 356-1, assigned to unit CO Capitano Aldo Li Greci, at Kantemirovka during the winter of 1942–43 (*Tony Holmes Collection*)

21° *Gruppo* remained at Odessa until April 1943 by which point it had just nine airworthy *Folgores*. These aircraft returned to Italy early the following month, with five unserviceable C.202s being left behind. Whilst assigned to 21° *Gruppo* on the Eastern Front, the *Folgores* had completed just 17 operational missions. One aircraft had been lost in combat and a second destroyed in an operational accident. No aerial victories had been achieved.

AEGEAN *FOLGORES*

A small number of C.202s also saw action over the Aegean from early 1943 with 154° *Gruppo Autonomo*, which had been posted to the theatre in May of the previous year. The unit's two *squadriglie* (395ª and 396ª) were equipped with CR.42s and G.50s, which were flown from Gadurra and Maritsa on the island of Rhodes. There was also a section of fighters based on nearby Kos.

Following a series of unsuccessful interceptions of RAF aircraft (principally Beaufighters, which were appreciably faster than the fighters assigned to 154° *Gruppo Autonomo*), unit CO Maggiore Delio Guizzon pleaded with the overall commander of Aegean forces, Generale Ulisse Longo, for C.202s in order to raise the morale of his men. The first seven *Folgores* reached Rhodes on 26 February 1943, and after initially being divided between the two *squadriglie,* they were grouped together within 396ª *Squadriglia* so as to ease the aircrafts' maintenance requirements.

The C.202s were involved in a number of inconclusive actions during March and April 1943, with *Folgore* pilots repeatedly encountering enemy aircraft – 39 times in April alone. However, the only clash that tallies with RAF loss records in this theatre prior to the Armistice came on 30 July, when two C.202s from 396ª *Squadriglia* engaged two Beaufighters from No 227 Sqn over Alimnia Island, west of Rhodes. One of the British aircraft was so badly damaged that it force-landed upon returning to the unit's airfield at El Magrun North, in Cyrenaica. The *Folgores* were also slightly damaged in the clash, after which the pilots involved claimed two 'Beauforts' destroyed.

With the engine of his C.202 already turning over, a pilot is helped into his fighter in late 1942 (*Archivio Ufficio Storico Stato Maggiore Esercito-Archivio Fotografico*)

On 8 September, when the Armistice came into effect, 154° *Gruppo Autonomo* had just eight aircraft on strength, six of which were airworthy. Two of these were on Kos, flown by Sottotenente Giuseppe Morganti and an unnamed NCO. Following the Armistice, most 396ª *Squadriglia* personnel initially sided with the Allies, who had launched operations intended to counter imminent action in-theatre by German forces. The unit played an active part in the island's doomed defence, culminating on 13 September with the downing of a Ju 88 reconnaissance aircraft by Tenente Morganti between Rhodes and Scarpanto.

Despite the efforts of Italo-British forces, the Germans had seized Kos by 4 October. They then turned their attention to Leros Island, which was again defended by a small Italo-British garrison. Convinced by German success to abandon the Allied cause, many 154° *Gruppo* pilots now joined the newly created *Repubblica Sociale Italiana* and its AR. The *gruppo* was then re-named the *Reparto Aereo Egeo* (RAE – Aegean Air Unit), and it again took up the fight against the Allies. The handful of C.202s, which had been adorned with Luftwaffe markings for tactical recognition purposes (despite the protestations of their Italian pilots), were tasked with escorting Ju 87s of SG 3 and Ju 88s of KGs 6 and 51.

The *Folgores* subsequently engaged RAF aircraft on a handful of occasions, including on 30 October 1943 when they intercepted Cyprus-based Beaufighters providing fighter cover for the British cruiser HMS *Aurora* and three destroyers – these vessels had been given the job of seeking out Axis warships in the Aegean. Four Beaufighters from No 227 Sqn sighted 17 Ju 88s escorted by what were identified as three C.202s from the RAE (these machines may have been Bf 109s from 9./JG 27). Although the bombers succeeded in badly damaging *Aurora*, four Ju 88s were lost to Beaufighters or anti-aircraft fire.

The Axis fighters then attacked the No 227 Sqn aircraft, with the rudder of one Beaufighter being badly damaged by what the crew stated was a 'C.202'. A second aircraft then got on the tail of the 'C.202', which broke off its attack and spiralled slowly away. Although no Italian pilots made any claims following this action, Unteroffizier Hannes Löffler of 9./JG 27 was credited with a Beaufighter kill.

Beaufighters and C.202s possibly clashed again on 15 November following the commencement of Operation *Taifun* by German forces two days earlier. Lasting just 72 hours, *Taifun* saw Italian and British troops defeated in their attempt to keep hold of Leros Island. On the 15th, Beaufighters from Nos 47 and 227 Sqns fought single-engined Axis fighters off Leros, with two of the aircraft being identified as 'C.202s with German insignia'. No 227 Sqn's Flt Lt Tommy Deck reported firing a short burst at a Macchi, which dropped its undercarriage and dived down to sea level to disengage. No Beaufighters were hit in return, despite being chased in the direction of the Turkish coast.

The RAE suffered its only fatality the following month when, on 14 December, Sergente Domenico Sancristoforo's C.202 crashed into the sea between Rhodes and Scarpanto. It is not clear why this happened, for no claims were made by Allied aircraft on that date. Sancristoforo was officially recognised as the first AR pilot to be killed in action. There were no further clashes between *Folgores* and Allied aircraft in the Aegean through to war's end.

CHAPTER FIVE

DEFENDING ITALIAN SOIL

By the time Tunisia fell to the Allies on 13 May 1943, *Folgore*-equipped units previously committed to operations in North Africa had been withdrawn to airfields on Sicily and Sardinia, as well as on the southern coastline of the Italian mainland. Some had been here since the autumn of 1942, and they had encountered an increasing number of RAF and USAAF medium and heavy bombers, escorted by large numbers of fighters, hitting military and industrial targets.

C.202 pilots had quickly found that their lightly armed fighters were ill suited to attacking USAAF B-17 and B-24 bomber streams. Furthermore, the only way they could survive the 'wall' of defensive fire thrown up by these American 'heavies' was to approach them head-on. However, this form of attack gave pilots only a brief firing window in which to inflict damage on their opponents.

Some units, like Palermo-based 377ª *Squadriglia*, had been attempting to defend Italian soil from Allied bombers well before Tunisia fell. Its pilot claimed a small number of heavy bombers destroyed, including on 3 February 1943 when B-24s, escorted by P-38s, attacked Palermo harbour. Future ace Tenente Luigi Torchio was credited with downing a Lightning, although he was wounded shortly thereafter when his C.202 was mortally damaged by another P-38. Squadronmates Sergente Leonzio Bicego and Sergente Maggiore Giordano Migliavacca attacked two 'four-engined' bombers during the same engagement, claiming them as probably

C.202s of 22° *Gruppo Autonomo* prepare to be refuelled and rearmed at Naples-Capodichino following a successful sortie in mid-1943. The smiling pilot in his flight suit in the centre of the photograph is eight-victory ace Tenente Orfeo Mazzitelli of 371ª *Squadriglia*, who is in conversation with an aviator from 356ª *Squadriglia* (note the numerals on his lifejacket) (*Aeronautica Militare-Fototeca Storica*)

On 3 February 1943, five-victory ace Tenente Luigi Torchio of 377ª *Squadriglia* claimed a P-38 destroyed near Palermo's Punta Zafferano. However, his C.202, MM7712 377-1, was damaged during the course of the engagement and the pilot was forced to belly land at Palermo-Boccadifalco airfield. Torchio is seen here in his flight suit, partially obscured by a member of the groundcrew, in conversation with his CO, Capitano Luigi Marcolin, who is crouching on the edge of the cockpit (*Aeronautica Militare-Fototeca Storica*)

destroyed. None were lost, however. This encounter was typical of the actions being fought at the time, with individual flights of four C.202s attempting to repel considerably larger formations of heavy bombers, and their substantial fighter escort.

Targets on the Italian mainland were also more frequently bombed from late 1942, with the port city of Naples being routinely attacked due to both its location and substantial naval base. In the vanguard of its defence was 22° *Gruppo Autonomo*, which had been sent from Sardinia to Capodichino airfield in late December 1942 expressly to defend Naples. Flying several different fighter types, including the C.202, its pilots came to be revered by Neapolitans for their bravery in action as they faced the growing might of the USAAF's Ninth Air Force.

Dubbed the 'Hunters of Vesuvius' by the local press, amongst the more successful aviators from 22° *Gruppo Autonomo* were Tenente Lorenzo Monaco (who, being a doctor, was nicknamed the 'flying obstetrician') and eight-victory ace Tenente Orfeo Mazzitelli of 371ª *Squadriglia*. Monaco's most successful day in the defence of Naples came on 11 January 1943 when he was at the controls of one of ten fighters (both C.200s and C.202s) scrambled to intercept eight approaching Liberators, split into two flights of four, which he misidentified as Flying Fortresses. His combat report following the engagement read as follows;

'Climbing in my C.202, I positioned myself behind and a little below the last bomber in the formation, aiming my guns at the space between the starboard inner engine and the fuselage. One "Fortress" was armed with 15 machine guns – four "Fortresses" arrayed in a lozenge-shaped formation could aim at least eight to ten, maybe 12, machine guns at me at once. Just as I opened fire, I saw my fighter "wrapped" with tracer. Lacking the will to resist this defensive fire, I dived away to starboard.

'Upon repositioning myself behind the bomber again, I spotted smoke starting to trail behind the port wing between the engine and the fuselage. Moments later, I saw flames. The "Fortress" banked to port and dropped out of formation. The blaze grew larger as the aircraft rolled away.

'I then throttled up once again and re-positioned myself behind and a little below the three remaining bombers. I aimed at the formation leader, and quickly spotted that it too was on fire. The stricken aircraft listed to port, while the two other bombers stayed in formation. The lead bomber exploded in mid-air like a firework, while my first victim continued to drop away in flames. With my ammunition virtually exhausted, I decided it was pointless chasing after the two remaining bombers, so I returned to base.'

Monaco's *Folgore* escaped unscathed from the one-sided clash. This was not the case on 15 February, however, when 16 B-24s again targeted Naples harbour. They were intercepted by 18 C.200s and C.202s of 22° *Gruppo,* which engaged the bombers for a full 30 minutes. In that time the Italian fighters were severely mauled by the gunners' return fire, with three *Folgores* being lost and two more badly damaged. A solitary Liberator was downed in return, a second was forced to crash land back at its base in Libya and three more were damaged.

Tenente Monaco was in action again on 1 March when 18 B-24s were detected approaching the Gulf of Naples. Scrambled with wingman Sergente Franco Sarasino, Monaco later recalled;

'Spotted four formations of six "Fortresses" coming in from the sea.

22° *Gruppo Autonomo*'s 'spauracchio' (scarecrow) insignia can just be made out on the fuselage band of this C.202 overflying the Mount Vesuvius area whilst defending Naples in 1943. *Folgores* adorned with this distinctive marking, created by eight-victory ace Sottotenente Giuseppe Biron in July 1941, were rarely photographed (*Aeronautica Militare-Fototeca Storica*)

Each formation took a different direction. I banked to the left and throttled up, losing sight of Sarasino in the process. Having originally served as a ground attack pilot with 22° *Gruppo*, I had been taught fighter tactics from veteran aviators that had joined 371ª *Squadriglia* after it had received C.202s for the defence of Naples. They had instructed me in how to attack bombers from above, the side and head-on.

'I tried to carry out a conventional attack from the rear, but as I hurled myself at a six-strong formation, the return fire aimed in my direction was lethal. In order to throw the gunners' aim off, I didn't pull up after my attack but continued to dive down. I then sighted another formation heading for me from the starboard side. Passing under this second formation, I pulled up steeply below them. In order not to fly into my target aircraft, I had to throttle back and push the nose of my fighter down, while also firing at the bomber's belly – which filled my windscreen! While firing, I saw a white-coloured smoke trail erupt from the stricken aircraft. However, upon diving sharply away from the bomber, my cockpit fogged up before I could see any flames.

'Disengaging from combat, I noticed black smoke trailing behind my C.202. This filled with me with such dread that I took off a glove and ran my hand between my bottom and my seat to feel if there was any heat. Fortunately, there was none, so I headed home.'

Monaco's Macchi had taken five hits, and he nursed the ailing fighter first to Torre del Greco and then on to Capodichino. Once on the ground, he was informed that spotters from the *Regia Marina* had seen a bomber plunge into the sea trailing white smoke. Monaco had achieved his third success over Naples.

Early April saw the Ninth Air Force's bombing campaign against Naples reach its climax, with a series of raids being flown. 22° *Gruppo*'s Tenente Orfeo Mazzitelli was in the thick of the action on the 4th when he claimed a B-24 destroyed for his second victory in the C.202. Six days later, 24 Liberators again targeted the port city, with 31 Italian fighters from three different units being scrambled to intercept them. Among the aircraft involved were seven C.202s from 22° *Gruppo* and 18 from 51° *Stormo*, which repeatedly attacked the Liberators and forced some of them to drop their bombloads early. Two C.202s were lost and

Having flown CR.32s during the Spanish Civil War and C.200s on the Eastern Front, Tenente Giuseppe 'Bepi' Biron (seen here with the 'spauracchio' insignia that he created) of 369ª *Squadriglia*, 22° *Gruppo Autonomo* was almost certainly the most successful C.202 pilot against the Lightning in the final weeks of the *Regia Aeronautica*. He was credited with three P-38s and a B-17 destroyed in the Naples area between 21 and 28 August 1943 (*Tony Holmes Collection*)

two more damaged. The B-24 gunners claimed two kills and two probables for no losses, although ten bombers were damaged.

Another attack by 20 B-24s on 11 April was again intercepted by 31 fighters from 22° *Gruppo* and 18 from 51° *Stormo*. The latter unit had a C.202 shot down and its pilot killed, while a single Liberator was destroyed and a second bomber badly damaged. The following day, 12 B-24s were intercepted by 26 Italian fighters, of which 18 were *Folgores* (12 from 51° *Stormo*). Tenente Mazzitelli was credited with a Liberator kill for his third victory in the C.202, although the USAAF reported damage to just one of its B-24s.

The final raid in April came on the 28th, with 25 B-24s being engaged by 20 fighters (all bar five of were *Folgores*) from 22° *Gruppo*. Italian pilots claimed four B-24s destroyed, one of which was credited to C.202 pilot Sergente Sergio Donati. Only one Liberator was destroyed, however, this aircraft being the last of ten B-24s lost during the course of 13 raids on Naples by the 98th and 376th BGs.

22° *Gruppo* continued to defend Naples from Capodichino through to the Armistice, its pilots claiming victories against USAAF bombers and, increasingly, escorting P-38 fighters. Eastern Front veteran Tenente Giuseppe 'Bepi' Biron of 369ª *Squadriglia* was perhaps the most successful C.202 pilot against the Lightning in the final weeks of the *Regia Aeronautica*, claiming three P-38s and a B-17 in the Naples area between 21 and 28 August.

A veteran fighter pilot, Biron had previously been credited with shared victories while flying C.200s against the Soviet air force in early 1942 – 22° *Gruppo* did not record individual successes at that time. An analysis of combat reports by historians indicate that Biron downed at least four aircraft, and possibly as many as six, whilst flying on the Eastern Front. By August 1943, individual victories were being officially recorded at unit level, with successful pilots receiving financial rewards; the level of the 'pay out' varied according to whether the aircraft destroyed was single-, twin- or multi-engined.

Tenente Mazzitelli had also remained active during the summer months, after claiming his fourth (B-24) and fifth (B-17) victories on 24 and 25 May, respectively. He was credited with another B-17 on 17 July, followed by P-38s on 30 August and 6 September. The latter victory was also the final success credited to 22° *Gruppo* before the Armistice.

ISLAND DEFENCE

During the Casablanca Conference of January 1943 between President Franklin D Roosevelt and Prime Minister Winston Churchill, and their respective Chiefs of Staff, the decision was taken to attack Sicily once Axis forces had been defeated in North Africa. Churchill, in particular, pushed for the invasion of Italy in an effort to relieve the pressure on Soviet forces on the Eastern Front.

Sicily was seen as the first step in this campaign, although the tiny island of Pantelleria, midway between Tunisia and Sicily, had to be neutralised first. Heavily fortified, with a 12,000-strong garrison and more than 100 coastal guns, Pantelleria provided Axis forces with defensive 'eyes' in this region thanks to the radar installations positioned on both it and nearby Lampedusa.

In the month prior to the fall of Tunisia, Pantelleria had been home to the first unit to receive C.205V *Serie I* (which lacked the wing-mounted MG 151 cannon) aircraft when 71ª *Squadriglia* of 17° *Gruppo*, 1° *Stormo* flew in from Sicily in early April. The *Veltros* were soon in action over the Strait of Sicily supporting the evacuation of Axis troops from Tunisia, pilots being tasked with protecting transport aircraft and naval vessels as best they could in the face of vastly superior Allied forces.

The first recorded action involving the aircraft took place over Pantelleria on 13 April when the airfield on the island was attacked by eight Spitfires. Six C.205Vs were scrambled in response, and these aircraft clashed with six more Spitfires that were providing high cover. The Italian pilots subsequently claimed two 'P-40s' shot down, although only one Spitfire was damaged. A C.205V was also damaged in return.

In what was probably the largest action fought by 1° *Stormo* during this period, 25 C.205Vs from 6° and 17° *Gruppi*, along with nine C.202s, attacked four squadrons of Spitfires on an offensive sweep 15 miles west of Pantelleria on 20 April. Following a fiercely contested dogfight, the Italian pilots claimed 14 Spitfires shot down for the loss of two C.205s, with two more Macchis damaged. Amongst those credited with a victory was 88ª *Squadriglia* ace Maresciallo Gianlino Baschirotto, who scored his sixth, and last, individual kill of the war. This assumed success by the *Regia Aeronautica* received considerable coverage in the Italian press, which emphasised the superiority of the new C.205V. In reality, not a single Spitfire had been lost.

Both 4° and 51° *Stormi* would also receive a few *Veltros* to fly alongside their C.202s during April, prior to both units being sent into action in the defence of Sicily the following month.

Five days prior to the surrender of Axis forces in Tunisia on 13 May, the Allies turned their attention to Pantelleria with the first in a series of largescale bombing raids. No fewer than 228 medium bombers and 13 bomb-carrying P-38s targeted the island on the 8th as a precursor to Operation *Corkscrew* – the invasion of Pantelleria. Three C.205Vs were damaged in the attack, after which most of the aircraft previously based there were sent back to Sicily. Only a *squadriglia* of C.202s from 151° *Gruppo* remained behind to provide direct defence. With insufficient underground shelters for its aircraft and continual bombing raids and shelling from Allied warships offshore, the *gruppo*, bar four C.202s, was evacuated to Sicily on 21 May.

On 11 June the Allies seized the island. During the final 11 days of fighting in defence of Pantelleria, a total of 57 German and Italian

Devastating Allied bombing raids on Pantelleria in mid-May 1943 forced the C.202s of 151° *Gruppo* to join 53° *Stormo* on Sicily. C.202 MM91956 368-1 – the personal mount of the CO of 368ª *Squadriglia*, Capitano Mario Ferrero – is seen here at readiness alongside other Macchis at Palermo-Boccadifalco airfield. On 8 June Capitano Ferrero was killed in action fighting USAAF P-40s near Pantelleria (*Author's Collection*)

aircraft had been shot down, a number of them C.202s and C.205Vs. Conversely, Anglo-American forces had lost 43 aircraft during the brief campaign.

The majority of the victories and losses involving C.202s and C.205Vs in the defence of Pantelleria came in the final three days of the brief campaign, when *gruppi* from Sicily-based 1° and 53° *Stormi* were thrown into action against large formations of heavily escorted USAAF medium and heavy bombers. *Folgore* and *Veltro* pilots claimed 21 victories (all Spitfires, bar three Bostons and a P-38) during three consecutive days of fighting, with 15 Macchi fighters shot down in return.

Most of the losses came on 10 June (the third anniversary of Italy's entry into World War 2), when the Allies mounted their heaviest bombing effort against Pantelleria. Nineteen separate raids were flown involving 550 aircraft, with 1500 tons of bombs being dropped on the island. C.202s from 151°, 153° and 161° *Gruppi* fought fierce battles with USAAF Spitfires from the 31st Fighter Group (FG) and P-40s from the 79th FG, these fighters escorting B-25s from the 12th and 340th BGs. Seven *Folgore* pilots were lost during the course of the day, including the CO of 151° *Gruppo*, Capitano Domenico Bevilacqua.

With the fall of Pantelleria, Allied attention now turned to Sicily. A number of attacks had already been carried out on the island from bases in North Africa and Malta, and Sardinia was also subjected to raids from USAAF and RAF medium bombers as the Allies attempted to confuse their Axis foes with respect to their next target for invasion.

One such mission against Sicily took place on 25 May, when 90 B-17s and 44 B-24s hit the port of Messina. Escorted by P-38s from the 1st FG, the bombers were intercepted by Bf 109s from JG 53 and C.202s and C.205s from 6°, 17°, 153° and 161° *Gruppi*, whose pilots claimed to have downed 14 four-engined bombers and a P-38. Amongst the successful pilots was Sergente Maggiore Fausto Fornaci of 161° *Gruppo*, who was credited with two B-17s destroyed. Only one bomber was downed, two force-landed and two others were also damaged. Three P-38s from the 1st FG were lost to enemy fighters.

Two days later, 26 B-26s from the 320th BG, escorted by 35 P-40s from the 325th FG, attacked Decimomannu airfield. They were intercepted by 14 C.202s and two C.205s from 20° *Gruppo*, and two P-38s and a P-40 were claimed as destroyed (only one P-40 was lost). Although the fighter escorts and Marauder gunners were credited with 13 victories between them, actual losses amounted to two C.202s and their pilots. One of the latter was Capitano Italo D'Amico, CO of 151ª *Squadriglia*.

These attacks continued to intensify in June as the Allies made preparation for the invasion of Sicily (codenamed Operation *Husky*) and, if all proceeded as planned, the conquest of the southern flank of 'Fortress Europe'. At the same time, the *Regia Aeronautica* prepared for the defence of Sicily, and on 1 July the *Aeronautica della Sicilia* had 166 fighters (of which 78 were serviceable) under its control on the island. The principal Macchi-equipped fighter units on Sicily were 4° *Stormo*, with its C.202s and C.205Vs of 9° and 10° *Gruppi* dispersed between Catania and Gerbini and their satellite airstrips, 21° *Gruppo Autonomo* at Chinisia, 161° *Gruppo Autonomo* (which also flew C.200s, CR.42s and ex-French D.520s) at Reggio Calabria and a flight of C.202s from 153° *Gruppo* charged with defending Palermo.

Sottotenente Felice Figus claimed four victories flying C.200s with 78ª *Squadriglia*, 13° *Gruppo*, 2° *Stormo* over Tunisia in the space of a month from December 1942 through to January 1943. Following his evacuation to Sicily, Figus was posted to C.202-equipped 374ª *Squadriglia*, which was assigned to 153° *Gruppo* at Palermo-Boccadifalco (*Federico Figus Family*)

SAI Ambrosini-built *Serie V* C.202s from 153° *Gruppo*'s 374ª *Squadriglia* taxi out at Palermo-Boccadifalco at the start of a mission in early June 1943. The aircraft closest to the camera has Tenente Felice Figus at the controls. It was destroyed on 30 June when Figus had to force-land three miles from Palermo-Boccadifalco after the C.202 was shot up by two P-38s of the 14th FG (*Federico Figus Family*)

Capitano Franco Lucchini was the *Regia Aeronautica*'s second-ranking ace of World War 2 with 21 victories to his credit – he also had a single victory from his service in the Spanish Civil War. Lucchini was killed leading 10° *Gruppo* in action over Sicily on 5 July 1943, his *Folgore* being hit by defensive fire from a formation of B-17s from the 99th BG (*USSMA*)

From 8 May to 11 June 1943, when Pantelleria surrendered, Axis fighters and fighter-bombers conducted a fierce battle with Allied air and naval forces. In this photograph, a C.202 of 53° *Stormo*, severely damaged in combat over the island, has been force-landed at Chinisia. In the background, three bomb-laden Fw 190s are in the process of taking off on a mission to attack Allied naval vessels supporting the Pantelleria campaign (*Author's Collection*)

Also at readiness were 60 fighters in central Italy, based halfway between Sardinia and Sicily at Ciampino-Roma, that could provide immediate defensive or offensive support to Sicilian units. These aircraft were assigned to 3° and 51° *Stormo*, controlling 22°, 160° and 24° *Gruppi* equipped with C.202s, C.205Vs, Re.2001s and Re.2005s. Other autonomous fighter units were dispersed at bases on Sardinia, and at Calabria, Puglia and Campania, from where they too would be available to defend Sicily whenever required. The Luftwaffe was also similarly prepared, with 350-400 aircraft committed to the defence of the island.

The Axis plan, although theoretically sound, was thrown into disarray by overwhelming Allied air power – as had been the case during Operation *Corkscrew*. Bombers hammered eastern and western airfields on Sicily for ten straight days and nights without respite from 2 July, rendering them practically unusable. These strikes forced the withdrawal of the shattered fighter units from western and central bases on the island, leaving the remnants concentrated on the plains near Catania.

On 4 and 5 July, *Folgores* and *Veltros* were heavily committed, with C.202s and C.205Vs from 4° *Stormo* alone flying 146 sorties on the 4th. Its pilots were credited with destroying nine P-38s, five Spitfires, four B-24s (these were, in fact, B-17s) and a B-25 for the loss of a C.202 and two C.205s. Sixteen more victories were scored the following day, but this time six *Folgores* – all from 4° *Stormo* – were shot down. Two of the three pilots killed on 5 July were the *Regia Aeronautica*'s second- and third-ranking aces Capitano Franco Lucchini and Sottotenente Leonardo Ferrulli, both from 10° *Gruppo*.

Lucchini, a veteran of the Spanish Civil War, had been made CO of the *gruppo* the previous month. Having claimed a Spitfire for his 22nd victory, Lucchini then went after a formation of B-17s from the 99th BG that was targeting Gerbini. In full view of his horrified wingmen, Lucchini's *Folgore* was caught in the bombers' deadly crossfire and the fighter fell away out of control. His body was found two days later, still entangled in the remains of his aircraft. Sergente Amleto Monterumici, who flew as a wingman to Lucchini, recalled how the ace boldly took on the enemy, even in the face of great odds;

'He was always ready to fight, and courageously sought out the enemy at every opportunity. As with a great number of fighter pilots, he was blessed with extraordinary eyesight, which meant he could spot his enemy and anticipate an attack. Although he was serious, withdrawn and occasionally timid, in the air he transformed himself into a frightening, aggressive fighter.'

Within minutes of Lucchini's demise, 21-victory ace and fellow Spanish Civil War veteran Leonardo Ferrulli had also been killed. Having shot

down a P-38 the previous day, Ferrulli was at the controls of one of 14 C.202s that had been scrambled from Reggio Calabria during the morning of 5 July to intercept B-17s over the Strait of Messina. Having claimed a Flying Fortress shot down (three fell to fighters), as well as an escorting P-38, Ferrulli was then reportedly seen engaging 30 enemy fighters over Sardi. Eventually forced to bail out of his badly damaged C.202, Ferrulli jumped too late and his parachute failed to deploy before he hit the ground.

Aside from the Axis fighters lost in the air on 5 July, many more had been destroyed on the ground at Catania and Gerbini airfields in raids that had seen 1400 tons of bombs dropped on Sicily. More aircraft were lost in follow-up attacks on eastern airfields on 8 July.

By the time Operation *Husky* was launched before dawn on 10 July 1943, the *Regia Aeronautica* had just 133 fighters (104 of which were C.202s and C.205Vs) left on Sicily. 4° *Stormo* had 48 *Folgores* and *Veltros* mainly at Finocchiara and San Salvatore, 21° *Gruppo Autonomo's* 21 C.202s were at Trapani-Chinisia, 153° *Gruppo Autonomo* had seven C.202s at Palermo and 161° *Gruppo Autonomo's* 18 C.202s were at Reggio Calabria. Only 49 of these aircraft were serviceable.

In response to the invasion, eight C.202s at 3° *Stormo* and ten C.205Vs from 51° *Stormo* were moved to the island from Cerveteri and Sardinia. In Italy, the *Regia Aeronautica's* invasion plans came into effect, with eight C.202s of 3° *Stormo* at Cerveteri and ten C.205Vs of 51° *Stormo* at Capoterra and Monserrato being part of the force quickly sent to Sicily. These aircraft had little impact on the Allies, whose Mediterranean Air Command now dominated the skies over the island following weeks of bombing. The Italians lost roughly 160 aircraft in the air and on the ground in the first few days following the landings, with 31 of them falling between 10 and 12 July alone.

With the airfields at Catania, Gerbini, Reggio Calabria, Crotone, Grottaglie and Palermo having been rendered unusable, the *Aeronautica della Sicilia* ordered all units at airfields in Calabria and Puglia to evacuate back to Italy on the 16th. Five days later, it too retreated to the mainland. This left just a handful of fighters on Sicily, including 12 C.202s from 155° *Gruppo*. These aircraft rarely ventured aloft in the final weeks of the defence of Sicily, with the island falling into Allied hands on 17 August following the departure of the remaining Italian and German defenders.

Although never invaded by the Allies, nearby Sardinia also felt the might of RAF and USAAF air power during the summer of 1943. One of the bloodiest actions for the Macchi fighter force defending the island took place on 22 July when 48 P-40s from the 325th FG on a sweep of southern Sardinia were intercepted by 21 C.202s and C.205Vs from 51° *Stormo's* 20° and 155° *Gruppi*.

Amongst the aircraft scrambled was the first *Veltro Serie III* delivered to a frontline unit, the fighter being armed with MG 151 20 mm cannon in the wings. Its pilot was ace Sergente Maggiore Ferruccio Serafini of 155°

Seven-victory ace Sergente Maggiore Ferruccio Serafini of 155° *Gruppo's* 378ª *Squadriglia* lost his life on 22 July 1943 fighting with Warhawks from the 325th FG over Sardinia. Flying the first *Veltro Serie III* delivered to a frontline unit, he shot a P-40 down, and then expended all of his remaining ammunition trying to destroy a second. Having resorted to ramming the Warhawk, Serafini bailed out too late from his stricken C.205V and was killed (*USSMA*)

C.205V MM9291 360-3 of 360ª *Squadriglia*, 155° *Gruppo*, 51° *Stormo* was photographed between missions at Monserrato in June 1943, the pilot's parachute draped over the rear fuselage and his harness resting on its port tailplane. One of the seat straps is also visible below the aerial mast, the groundcrew having moved it out of the way in order to facilitate the rapid occupation of the cockpit by the pilot in the event of a short-notice scramble (*Tony Holmes Collection*)

Gruppo's 378ª *Squadriglia*, who shot down a P-40 for his sixth victory. He then chased down a second Warhawk, but exhausted his ammunition before he could destroy the USAAF fighter. Having resorted to ramming his opponent, Serafini was forced to bail out of the C.205V when the fighter lost part of its wing. Having abandoned his aircraft too late, the ace was killed when he hit the ground before his parachute had fully deployed.

Serafini was one of three Macchi pilots from 51° *Stormo* lost in this action, with three more fighters being badly shot up and one pilot wounded. Although ten P-40s had been credited to the *gruppi*, only two had in fact been shot down.

The final largescale action to be fought between Allied fighters and Sardinia-based units took place on 2 August when P-38s of the 14th FG tangled with C.205Vs from 20° and 155° *Gruppi*. All three units were protecting flying boats sent to retrieve downed airmen, the USAAF fighters covering an OA-10 Catalina and the Macchis protecting a Z.506B. The latter was brought down in a mid-air collision with a USAAF P-40 near the Sardinian port of Cagliari, prompting the OA-10's despatch in search of survivors. Upon spotting wreckage, the Catalina landed, but the flying boat had its port propeller knocked off by a wave when it tried to take off again.

While the escorting Macchis and Lightnings clashed overhead, two C.205Vs broke away and strafed the OA-10, which soon sank. One of the attacking pilots was ace Maresciallo Ennio Tarantola of 20° *Gruppo*, who also claimed two P-38s destroyed. A total of 12 Lightnings were credited to C.205V pilots from 51° *Stormo* in two actions on the afternoon of 2 August, although none were lost. The P-38 pilots claimed four 'Me 109s' destroyed and three damaged in return. Only one C.205V was destroyed, resulting in the death of ace Maresciallo Pietro Bianchi from 20° *Gruppo*. He had fallen victim to a Lightning just moments after claiming his fifth kill.

DEFENDING THE MAINLAND

In a repeat of the dogged defence of Naples by 22° *Gruppo* detailed at the start of this chapter, Italian fighter units (mainly equipped with C.202s and a small number of C.205Vs) attempted to protect cities like Turin, Milan, Genoa, La Spezia and, of course, Rome, from Allied bombers between the spring of 1943 and 8 September. Emasculated *stormi*, which had been decimated over Sicily, coped as best they could with the situation, claiming a good number of Allied aircraft destroyed – more than 275 were credited to fighter pilots, the vast majority of which were flying *Folgores* and *Veltros*.

With its 20 mm cannon armament, the *Serie III* C.205V proved quite effective against Allied bombers targeting the Italian mainland. However, due to the fact that only around 70 *Serie III* airframes had been completed by Macchi prior to the Armistice, the aircraft was never available in sufficient numbers to fully equip a *stormo*. This meant that

A *Veltro* serving with 3° *Stormo*, based at Cerveteri, northwest of Rome, has its engine warmed up. One of around a dozen *Serie III* C.205Vs issued to the unit, the fighter's wing-mounted MG 151 20 mm cannon are clearly visible (*Aeronautica Militare-Fototeca Storica*)

frontline units had to assign what few *Veltros* they had to their best pilots.

This was indeed the case with 3° *Stormo*, whose 18° and 23° *Gruppi* saw more action in the defence of Rome than virtually any other fighter units of the *Regia Aeronautica* in the weeks leading up to the Armistice. Each *gruppo*, based at Cerveteri, northwest of the Italian capital, was issued with around a dozen *Serie III* aircraft to fly alongside C.202s and, in 23° *Gruppo*'s case, a few Bf 109G-6s.

For 3° *Stormo*, the leading lights of the defence of Rome were Tenente Franco Bordoni Bisleri and Sergente Maggiore Luigi Gorrini, both of whom had served with 18° *Gruppo* since 1939. The aces had returned to action in July 1943 following extended spells out of the cockpit following a car accident (Bordoni Bisleri) and an eye injury (Gorrini). As befitted their ace status, both men routinely flew the C.205V into action through to the Armistice.

Involved in incessant interceptions, Bordoni Bisleri claimed six B-17s and a B-26 destroyed (some of these were shared victories) between 30 July and 5 September to take his final tally to 19. Gorrini proved even more successful, being credited with four B-24s, four P-38s, a B-17 and two Spitfires destroyed through to 31 August, when, shortly after claiming his last Spitfire, he was injured after force-landing his *Veltro* near Naples. Following several weeks in hospital, Gorrini would join the AR and claim a further four victories in the C.205V between January and June 1944 to take his final tally to 19.

Sergente Maggiore Luigi Gorrini survived the war with 19 victories to his name, all bar two of which had been claimed in C.202s and C.205Vs. Having been credited with 15 kills (11 of them in the defence of the Italian mainland) whilst serving with 85ª *Squadriglia*, 18° *Gruppo*, 3° *Stormo*, Gorrini fought on with the AR and claimed a further four victories flying the C.205V with 1° *Gruppo Caccia* (*USSMA*)

Three days after Gorrini was hospitalised, Allied forces came ashore along the Calabrian coast at Reggio Calabria, Gallico and Catone as part of Operation *Baytown*. Between then and the announcement of the Armistice of Cassibile on 8 September, C.202 and C.205V pilots claimed just eight victories. Only two *Folgores* and two *Veltros* were lost during the same period, these low numbers reflecting how few Italian fighters now remained airworthy. Indeed, 3° *Stormo* could muster only 17 C.202s and four C.205Vs and 22° *Gruppo* just nine *Folgores* when the Allies' made public the signing of the Armistice, which had taken place five days earlier.

On 9 September, Allied forces landed between Salerno and Paestum, south of Naples on the west coast of Italy, to signal the start of Operation *Avalanche*. Italy was effectively split in two, with the Germans and Italian Fascists fighting on in the north of the country.

CHAPTER SIX

AFTER THE ARMISTICE

Mirroring the split in Italy in the wake of the Armistice, the air force also broke up into two factions, which, in many respects, were very similar. Indeed, it often appeared as if they were only divided by the insignia they carried on their respective aircraft – the pre-Fascist roundel in the south and the Italian flag, with fasces, in the north. The men on either side drew their heritage from a common history, and as in the days of the *Regia Aeronautica*, pilots and groundcrews struggled on with poor equipment and little logistical support.

At the time of the Armistice, the majority of what remained of the *Regia Aeronautica* was based in the central and northern regions of the Italian peninsula, where it had gradually retreated under the constant pressure of Anglo-American air power. With the announcement of the Armistice, such geographical locations facilitated the capture of many aircraft by the Germans. With a substantial number of units in the south now lacking any equipment, most, but not all, opted simply to disband.

MACCHIS IN THE SOUTH

When the Armistice came into effect, the only C.202-equipped units in southern Italy were 21° *Gruppo* at Manduria and Gioia del Colle, 4° *Stormo*, with its 9° *Gruppo* at Gioia del Colle and 10° *Gruppo* at Castrovillari, and

Sardinia-based 51° *Stormo*, with its 155° *Gruppo* at Milis and Case Zeppera and 13° *Gruppo* at Venafiorita. Pilots loyal to King Victor Emmanuel III also managed to fly six C.202s and around 50 C.205Vs from airfields in German-held territory and escape south.

Although the new Italian government led by Maresciallo Pietro Badoglio refused to declare war on its former ally Germany until 13 October 1943, Italian fighter pilots in the south flew a limited number of combat missions in protection of southern Italy immediately after the Armistice was announced. Amongst the pilots to have a close shave with their former Luftwaffe allies was Tenente Alessandro Mettimano, CO of 10° *Gruppo*'s 84ª *Squadriglia*;

'On 9 September all the Macchi 205s of my *squadriglia*, along with the other 4° *Stormo* aircraft, moved to Gioia del Colle from Castrovillari. Here, in accordance with Maresciallo Badoglio's proclamation of the previous evening, we had fighters readied on alert in case German aircraft tried to attack the airfield. We were determined to defend the base, and the Apulian skies, from any aggression by the enemy.

'I flew the first scramble with my Macchi 205 on the morning of 13 September. During the course of the mission, which lasted 45 minutes, I intercepted a Messerschmitt 109G that was approaching the airfield at nearby Lecce. Soon spotting the aircraft, I positioned myself on its tail for an attack. It was then that I clearly saw the face of the German pilot, who, realising my presence, had turned to look at me. Perhaps he was one of the many aviators with whom I had served alongside as allies in the skies of North Africa and Sicily.

'Rather than opening fire, I signalled with my hand for him to leave. He understood perfectly. Seeing that he couldn't take the initiative due my Macchi being immediately behind him, cannons trained, he throttled up and headed northwards. I didn't want to shoot him down, as we had been told to react only if attacked.'

Tenente Mettimano had intercepted a Bf 109G-6 from I./JG 77, which flew six reconnaissance missions over Apulian airfields on 13 September.

Not all encounters ended so harmoniously, with the Germans executing any Italian aviators they captured who were loyal to the King as 'rebels' due to the Badoglio government's refusal to declare war on the Third Reich. Such a fate befell Sottotenente Carlo Negri of 4° *Stormo* on 21 September when his C.205V was shot down by Flak while overflying Koritza airfield in Albania en route to dropping a message to Italian troops cut off behind German lines in the Balkans.

By coincidence, on the same day Sottotenente Negri was executed, *Regia Aeronautica* aircraft aligned with the Allies returned to displaying the red-white-green roundels on both the wings and fuselage in place of the fascist fasces.

C.205s were in action once again over Albania on 25 September when nine Macchi fighters from 4° *Stormo* strafed German landing craft off the coast. The aircraft were in turn bounced by two Bf 109s from IV./JG 27, one of which was shot down by Capitano Emanuele Annoni off Corfu for his ninth, and final, victory of the war – this was also his only kill against the Luftwaffe.

C.205V *Serie III* MM92214 was used by ace Maggiore Prince Carlo Maurizio Ruspoli di Poggio Suasa (seen here in the sunglasses) when he undertook a propaganda leaflet-dropping mission over German-occupied Rome on 6 October 1943. He was accompanied by fellow 4° *Stormo* ace Capitano Luigi Mariotti in MM92216. Both aircraft had leaflets packed into the cavity between the flaps and the upper wing surface. Once over Rome, the pilots selected flaps down and the leaflets dropped away (*Aeronautica Militare-Fototeca Storica*)

By the end of September there were just 17 *Folgores* (six airworthy) and an undisclosed number of C.205Vs on Apulian airfields, with six more C.202s (only four of which were serviceable) on Sardinia.

On 6 October, 4° *Stormo* aces Maggiore Prince Carlo Maurizio Ruspoli di Poggio Suasa and Capitano Luigi Mariotti were tasked with flying over Rome, which had been occupied by German troops, on a leaflet drop. Taking off from Foggia-Palata airfield and heading straight for the Italian capital at low-level, they released their leaflets over an area stretching from the historical Milvian Bridge to Porta San Paolo.

Following the declaration of war against Nazi Germany on 13 October, the Badoglio government was accorded Co-Belligerent, but not full ally, status. The Italian Co-Belligerent *Regia Aeronautica* (as it was unofficially named by the Allies) was duly formed, and shortly thereafter 4° *Stormo* commenced operations over Yugoslavia in support of the Italian Co-Belligerent *Venezia* and *Taurinense* army divisions.

The Allies had wisely prohibited the Co-Belligerent *Regia Aeronautica* from conducting further operations over Italian territory so as to avoid fratricidal encounters with the AR. Most airfields in the south had been requisitioned by Allied fighter and bomber units in any case, leaving Italian pilots in the south to congregate primarily at Lecce. Macchis would fly from Lecce-Galatina, Foggia-Palata, Campomarino-Nuova and Yugoslav-held Vis Island, in the Adriatic Sea.

4° *Stormo* duly became the *Raggruppamento Caccia* on 15 October following its reorganisation along the lines of an Allied fighter wing – aside from controlling the *Folgores* and *Veltros* of 4° *Stormo* (9° and 10° *Gruppi*), its numbers were bolstered by the inclusion of aircraft from 8° and 21° *Gruppi*. Upon its formation, the *Raggruppamento Caccia* had 24 C.202s (18 serviceable) and an undisclosed number of C.205Vs on strength. Commanded by Tenente Colonnello Duilio Fanali, the *Raggruppamento Caccia's* Macchi fighters would provide escorts for more than 500 supply sorties flown by the Allies in 1943–44 in support of Yugoslav partisans and Italian troops, the latter isolated in German-controlled areas of the Balkans. Ground attack missions were also flown, often at the very limit of the fighters' modest range.

The first aerial success enjoyed by the *Raggruppamento Caccia* came on 23 October, when two C.205Vs of 10° *Gruppo* flown by aces Maresciallo Alessandro Bladelli and Tenente Giuseppe Ferazzani shot down a Ju 52/3m over Berane, in Yugoslavia. On 19 November a mixed force of ten C.202s and 12 C.205Vs strafed Podgorica airfield, 90 miles southwest of Berane, shooting up five Bf 109s and four Ju 52/3ms. The target was defended by intense Flak, which hit three *Folgores*. One C.202 from 21° *Gruppo* had a hole shot in its main fuel tank, and the aircraft crashed just short of the runway at Lecce

when the fighter ran out of fuel. Capitano Trento Carotti, CO of 386ª *Squadriglia*, suffered grave injuries and later died in hospital.

As of 31 December, the *Raggruppamento Caccia*'s 27 C.202s (21 of which were serviceable) and C.205Vs were divided among 4° and 51° *Stormi* at Lecce. By now, the Co-Belligerent *Regia Aeronautica Servizio Tecnico Caccia* was really struggling to locate spare parts for the Macchi fighters. Italy's primary aviation manufacturers were all located in the north within German-occupied territory, ruling out the acquisition of new parts. This grave situation was further compounded when the Allies requisitioned the handful of aviation-related industrial centres in the south for their own needs – the Alfa Romeo engine plant at Pomigliano d'Arco, for example, was taken over for the servicing of British Army transport vehicles.

This left the Co-Belligerent *Regia Aeronautica* with little option but to scour airfields used by the pre-Armistice *Regia Aeronautica* – some of which were as far away as North Africa – for useable parts that could be stripped off dumped and battle-damaged aircraft. This effort soon bore fruit, and resulted in around 30 C.202s being converted by the *Servizio Tecnico Caccia* and *Aeronautica Sannita* into C.205s through the substitution of the former's DB 601 engine with a DB 605.

On 13 January 1944, 4° *Stormo* transferred 10° and 12° *Gruppi* north to Foggia-Palata, leaving 51° *Stormo* at Lecce-Leverano following its move from Sardinia on 25–26 December 1943. In order for the latter unit to undertake long-range sorties over the Balkans from southern Italy, at least 18 *Serie III* C.205Vs were rebuilt as *Grande Autonomia* (Long Range) aircraft, with 220-litre fuel tanks replacing the cowl-mounted machine guns and their ammunition. This left the fighters with only two wing-mounted 20 mm cannon. Aside from the *Serie III Grande Autonomia* aircraft, some *Serie I Veltros* were also modified into C.205S *Scortas*, allowing them to carry two underwing 100/150-litre drop tanks and keep their full armament.

Following almost three months of little activity due to a shortage of aircraft and the onset of poor winter weather, 4° *Stormo* was in action once again on 8 February when six C.205s attacked targets in Dubrovnik.

Tenente Colonnello Duilio Fanali, CO of the *Regia Aeronautica*'s 155° *Gruppo Caccia* and then leader of 51° *Stormo* of the Co-Belligerent *Regia Aeronautica*, poses with a unit mascot alongside a C.202 bearing the nickname *Principessa* (princess) on its cowling. This aircraft was subsequently passed on to 208ª *Squadriglia*, 101° *Gruppo*, 5° *Stormo*, where it became the personal mount of Capitano Giorgio Gasperoni (*Aeronautica Militare-Fototeca Storica*)

Opposed by heavy German Flak, the C.205V of seven-victory ace Capitano Ranieri Piccolomini Clementini was struck by shrapnel, wounding the pilot in the leg.

On 19 March, six C.202s from 51° *Stormo* targeted a Flak battery at Lapad, near Dubrovnik. An accurate attack by the lead Macchi caused ammunition to explode so violently that the second C.202 following close behind was severely damaged by shell splinters. Sottotenente Adolfo Roesler Franz managed to nurse his fighter out over the Adriatic Sea before he was forced to bail out 45 miles off the Dalmatian coast. Roesler Franz's body was never found.

Flak batteries in Yugoslavia continued to take a toll on Co-Belligerent *Regia Aeronautica* Macchi fighters in April. On the 11th, the C.205V flown by 4° *Stormo*'s Tenente Mario Mecatti was hit while he was strafing targets near Hum. The pilot bailed out just south of Trnovica, and with the help of Yugoslav partisans, he eventually reached Vis Island and was returned to his unit the following month. On 13 April Tenente Tullio Martinelli of 51° *Stormo* was participating in an offensive over Korcula Island, off the coast of Yugoslavia, when his C.202 was struck by Flak. He bailed out minutes later near neighbouring Lagosta Island and was soon rescued.

German Flak was not the only hazard facing pilots of the Co-Belligerent *Regia Aeronautica* at this time. They also had to contend with poor weather conditions and the mechanical vagaries of their ageing Macchi fighters. On 4 May five C.205Ss of 4° *Stormo* had been tasked with escorting 11 Z.1007bis undertaking a supply drop for Italian troops in Yugoslavia. Two of the fighters had to return early due to mechanical problems, with Sottotenente Edgardo Larsimont Pergameni being forced to bail out ten miles northeast of Lecce-Leverano when his engine finally failed. Despite an intensive search, he was never found.

A similar fate befell Tenente Mario Melis of 51° *Stormo* eight days later. He and a wingman had taken off in their C.202s from Lecce-Leverano on a weather reconnaissance mission over Podgorica, only to then get lost in thick haze 40 miles from the airfield. Melis failed to return to base, being listed as missing in action.

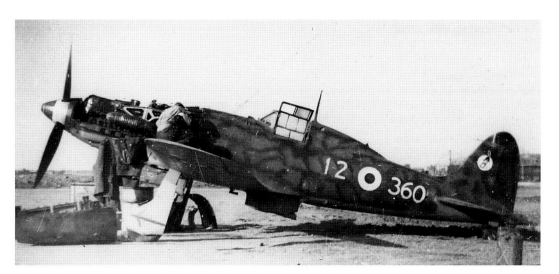

Painted in full Co-Belligerent *Regia Aeronautica* colours and markings (the roundel was reinstated on 21 September 1943), C.202 12-360 of 360ª *Squadriglia*, 155° *Gruppo*, 51° *Stormo* has its engine fettled at Lecce in late 1943. This aircraft was one of 27 *Folgores* (21 of which were serviceable) and *Veltros* then on strength with the *Raggruppamento Caccia* and divided between 4° and 51° *Stormi* (*Tony Holmes Collection*)

In June, C.202s from both 4° and 51° *Stormi* were handed over to 5° *Stormo* (composed of 8°, 101° and 102° *Gruppi*). 51° *Stormo,* waiting to be re-equipped with Spitfire VB/Cs, temporarily flew C.205Vs only, while 4° *Stormo* replaced its *Folgores* with P-39 Airacobras.

Following another extended period of little action, Co-Belligerent *Regia Aeronautica* Macchis engaged German Flak batteries once again on 16 July, resulting in the loss of the C.205V flown by Tenente Giovanni Franchini near Susak Island. The CO of 21° *Gruppo*'s 351ª *Squadriglia*, Franchini was rescued by partisans. Two *Folgores* were also lost that day when a pair of fighters from 5°

A well-weathered C.202 displays its recently applied roundels whilst on a mission from Lecce in early 1944. The national markings were painted over the wing fasces that had previously been worn by the *Folgore* during its service with the *Regia Aeronautica* (*Philip Jarrett Collection*)

Stormo's 102° *Gruppo* ran out of fuel and had to ditch near Vis Island. Tenente Silvio Leonesio was killed and Sottotenente Aldo Dagnino was found by partisans, having suffered injuries when ditching his C.202.

21° *Gruppo* lost another C.205V to Flak on 3 August during a strafing attack on Hutovo railway station. Sergente Maggiore Filippo Baldin bailed out and escaped capture with the help of partisans, returning to his unit 22 days later.

On 16 August the Macchi units moved from Nuova to Leverano airfield, commencing operations from their new base two days later. The first loss to Flak that month occurred exactly one week later when the 155° *Gruppo* C.205V of Sottotenente Giovanni Mancina was hit while strafing Porto Palermo, on the Albanian coast. The pilot bailed out near Santi Quaranta and, again with the assistance of partisans, returned to his unit four days later. 8° *Gruppo*'s Sergente Umberto Canali was not so lucky on 28 August when his C.202 was brought down by Flak over Albania, the pilot becoming a PoW.

More losses to ground fire and poor weather followed in September, as the Macchi fighters continued to harass German troop movements in Yugoslavia, Albania and Greece. On the 13th, the C.205S of 21° *Gruppo*'s Sottotenente Vittorio Sigismondi was hit by Flak while attacking a lorry. The fighter rolled onto its back and crashed near Metsovo, in Greece, before the pilot could bail out. Four days later, two C.202s of 101° *Gruppo* set off from Lecce-Leverano on an offensive patrol over the Koritza area. Whilst still crossing the Adriatic, wingman Sergente Maggiore Aldrovandi saw his leader, Tenente Carlo Graziani, dive away steeply into a bank of cloud. Graziani was never seen again.

On 24 September, two more C.202s from 101° *Gruppo* departed Lecce-Leverano on a routine armed reconnaissance mission to Doljana, in Yugoslavia, in search of enemy motor transports. Tenenti Socrate Peroni and Crisanto Venditti failed to return to base, being listed as missing in action. An RAF Spitfire pilot reported having sighted a fighter aircraft of an unknown type crashing in flames into the sea at around the time the *Folgore* pilots should have been returning to Lecce-Leverano.

With C.202 and C.205V numbers slowly dwindling, Co-Belligerent *Regia Aeronautica* units were involved in fewer and fewer missions over the Balkans. Although no examples were lost in October, 155° *Gruppo*'s 378ª *Squadriglia* suffered the Macchi fighters' final two combat casualties in November. On the 16th, the C.205V of Tenente Osvaldo Bartolozzi was hit by Flak over Albania. The aircraft was nursed back to Lecce-Leverano, where Bartolozzi carried out a successful forced landing. Four days later, Tenente Alberto Ballista became the last Macchi pilot of the Co-Belligerent *Regia Aeronautica* to be brought down by Flak when he force-landed near Shegas, in Albania, after his C.205V was hit north of Alessio. Wounded by shell fragments, he successful evaded capture thanks to the help of partisans.

Despite the war-weary condition of its surviving Macchi fighters, 5° *Stormo* continued to undertake escort missions for both bomber and transport aircraft until 26 December, when its *Folgores* were withdrawn from frontline service due to targets in Yugoslavia now being beyond the range of the C.202. It continued to operate C.205Vs through to VE Day, however, although little to no action was seen with these aircraft in the final six months of the war.

MACCHIS IN THE NORTH

In northern Italy, where the pro-German, fascist, *Repubblica Sociale Italiana* (RSI) had been established under the leadership of Mussolini, an agreement was reached in October 1943 between the *Sottosegretario per l'Aeronautica* (Undersecretary for the Air Force), one-legged ace Tenente Colonnello Ernesto Botto, and the Luftwaffe commander-in-chief in Italy, Generalfeldmarschall Wolfram von Richthofen (who led *Luftflotte* 2), for the creation of a temporary air force nucleus. Botto gave the new air arm the name *Aeronautica Repubblicana*, to which was added the word *Nazionale* in June 1944.

To begin with, aircrew assigned to the AR were those members of the *Regia Aeronautica* who had not escaped to the south when the Armistice came into effect. They were all volunteers (indeed, only three aviators deserted and flew south following the creation of the RSI) that had been deeply shocked by the announcement of the Armistice and the rapidity with which the political will to fight had collapsed. Angered by the fragmentation of the Italian nation, for many in the *Regia Aeronautica* their only stable points of reference were their own flying units and the comrades they served with. Furthermore, most AR pilots had families still living in northern Italy, which was being relentlessly attacked by Allied bombers.

Paramount amongst the many problems facing the RSI's new air arm was a solution to the difficult relationship the Italian forces now had with their wary German allies, who viewed them solely as a subordinate partner for the provision of labour and resources. As an example of this mentality, while the AR was struggling to form and equip its own autonomous units, the Germans requisitioned more than 1000 Italian aircraft of all types.

This situation was only resolved on 31 December 1943 when II./JG 77 handed back 22 C.205Vs. These aircraft were issued to 1° *Gruppo Caccia*, which had initially formed at Turin-Mirafiori airfield on 15 November under the command of Maggiore Luigi Borgogno. The group consisted of

C.205V MM92212 was the first aircraft delivered to 1° *Gruppo Caccia* by II./JG 77 to feature Italian markings, the fighter still bearing the yellow horizontal bar and individual numeral applied by its previous owner. Assigned to Capitano Marco Marinone, CO of 2ª *Squadriglia*, 1° *Gruppo Caccia*, in January 1944, the fighter saw early combat with the AR from Lagnasco (*Tony Holmes Collection*)

1ª *Squadriglia 'Asso di Bastoni'* (Ace of Clubs), 2ª *Squadriglia 'Vespa Arrabbiata'* (Angry Wasp) and 3ª *Squadriglia 'Arciere'* (Archer), led by Capitani Adriano Visconti, Marco Marinone and Pietro Calistri, respectively. A further 36 C.202s would be supplied to 3° *Gruppo* for use as training aircraft for future frontline pilots.

From 15 December, 1° *Gruppo Caccia* operated from Lagnasco airfield, 30 miles south of Turin. Nineteen days later, on 3 January 1944, Capitano Visconti led nine *Veltros* aloft as 1ª *Squadriglia* saw the *gruppo*'s first action. B-17s from the Fifteenth Air Force's 5th Bombardment Wing (BW), escorted by P-38s from the 14th FG, had been detected approaching Turin, and the C.205Vs were scrambled along with Bf 109Gs from II./JG 77.

A fierce dogfight then took place between the *Veltro* pilots and their USAAF counterparts in the Lightnings, Capitano Visconti choosing to disperse the escorting fighters, rather than attacking the bombers. Ordering his pilots to dive on the P-38s from an altitude of 31,000 ft, they took full advantage of their superior height to claim three Lightnings shot down and a fourth as a probable. The first victory for the AR was credited to Sergente Maggiore Francesco Cuscunà, with Capitano Visconti claiming a P-38 for his seventh confirmed victory and the third Lightning falling to Sottotenente Remo Lugari. The probable was claimed by Sottotenente Giovanni Sajeva, and the wreckage of this fighter was later found in the Italian Alps. All of the 1ª *Squadriglia* aircraft involved returned to base unscathed.

The 14th FG reported the loss of two P-38s to 'Macchi 202s'. II./JG 77 also claimed two Lightning victories. Regardless of whether the AR or Luftwaffe units had downed the P-38s, the results of this mission boosted the morale of the 1° *Gruppo Caccia* pilots.

On 24 January the *gruppo* moved from Lagnasco to Campoformido, near Udine in northeastern Italy. The location of its new base would give 1° *Gruppo Caccia* a better chance of intercepting Fifteenth Air Force heavy bombers heading from southern Italy to targets in Austria and southeastern Germany. The unit also received more C.205Vs at this time, a small number of new-build fighters emerging from the Macchi factory at Varese through to April 1944, when it was all but destroyed by Allied heavy bombers.

The *Veltros'* frontline service with the AR effectively lasted until August 1944, when 1° *Gruppo Caccia* was grounded for several months after the Luftwaffe tried to take direct control of all Italian units. When it resumed frontline operations at year-end, the C.205Vs had been replaced by Bf 109Gs supplied by the Luftwaffe. However, in the first seven months of the year, *Veltros* were very much in the thick of the fighting as the Fifteenth Air Force focused on knocking out Axis airfields in northern Italy.

1° *Gruppo Caccia's* first action of note from Campoformido took place on 30 January when 16 C.205Vs were scrambled to intercept 63 B-24s from the 449th and 450th BGs, escorted by 60 P-47 Thunderbolts from the 325th FG and a large number of P-38s from the 1st, 14th and 82nd FGs. The USAAF bombers were heading for airfields at Udine, Villaorba, Maniago, Lavariano and Campoformido.

In the subsequent air battle, which took place between Casarsa and Pordenone, the AR pilots claimed the destruction of a B-24 (with a second bomber as a probable) and four P-47s for the loss of three C.205Vs and two pilots shot down over Campoformido. Those killed were 1ª *Squadriglia* CO Capitano Marco Marinone, who was lost in an uneven fight with a formation of Thunderbolts, and five-victory CR.42 nightfighter ace Tenente Luigi Torchio. Fellow ace Maresciallo Carlo Magnaghi claimed two P-47s between Grado and Palmanova, while Tenente Giuseppe Re destroyed a third Thunderbolt prior to having to break off the fight and bail out of his badly damaged *Veltro*. A fourth Thunderbolt exploded after being hit by 15-victory ace Sergente Maggiore Luigi Gorrini.

The 325th FG recorded the loss of two P-47s, with two more being damaged. The Thunderbolts identified their opponents as 'MC.202s', and it appears that Lt F E Suehle was responsible for the death of Tenente Torchio, whose demise was witnessed by fellow ace Tenente Carlo Cucchi.

Sottotenente Natalino Stabile and Sergente Maggiore Aldo Burei succeeded in breaking through the escorts and repeatedly striking a B-24 from the 449th BG, which recorded that four Liberators were damaged by fighters. Stabile then attacked a lone bomber (again from the 449th BG), which he managed to shoot down into the Laguna di Grado. The 449th BG lost three B-24s during the course of this mission.

Despite 1° *Gruppo Caccia's* spirited defence of the AR airfields, the Liberators succeeded in bombing Campoformido. Here, 27 C.205Vs were damaged, three of them seriously, although the runway remained partially in use.

The following day, Sergente Maggiore Gorrini claimed an F-5 Lightning photo-reconnaissance aircraft shot down over Lake

C.205V *Serie III* MM92272 6-1 of 1ª *Squadriglia*, 1° *Gruppo Caccia* was photographed at Campoformido in early 1944. The *'Asso di Bastoni'* playing card marking on the nose of the fighter was one of several emblems previously used by the *Regia Aeronautica* to be appropriated by *squadriglie* serving with the AR from late 1943 *(Philip Jarrett Collection)*

Comacchio for his 17th victory, although no such loss was recorded by the USAAF.

31 January also saw Campoformido targeted once again when 41 B-24s from the 449th and 450th BGs dropped 29,000 fragmentation bombs on several airfields in the Udine area. A number of aircraft were severely damaged, as was the base infrastructure at Campoformido. Intercepting C.205Vs were unable to penetrate the strong fighter escort provided by the 325th FG, and Sottotenente Luciano Cipiciani was killed when his *Veltro* was shot down.

Campoformido would be bombed five times between 30 January and 18 March, the airfield being targeted by around 600 B-17s and B-24s. They would drop 600 tons of bombs and 30,000 fragmentation bombs, destroying eight C.205Vs and damaging a further 36 fighters. The wide dispersal of *Veltros* in well-protected blast pens meant that 1° *Gruppo Caccia* suffered comparatively light losses during these raids. The airfield infrastructure had, however, taken a pounding.

On 23 February Bf 109Gs from JG 77 misidentified 20 C.205Vs from 1° *Gruppo Caccia* patrolling between Fiume and Trieste. The lead Macchi flown by *gruppo* commander Maggiore Luigi Borgogno was badly shot up, forcing him to take to his parachute. Borgogno struck the fighter's rudder as he departed the aircraft, suffering serious injuries in the process. He was temporarily replaced by Capitano Adriano Visconti, who in turn handed the leadership of 1ª *Squadriglia* over to Tenente Giuseppe Robetto.

1° *Gruppo Caccia* was scrambled in strength on 11 March, with 36 C.205Vs being sent aloft to intercept B-17s from the 2nd and 97th BGs as they passed through the Veneto skies en route to the Padua marshalling yards. The bombers were escorted by 57 P-47s from the 325th FG. A fierce battle ensued as the AR fighters attempted to get at the B-17s. The Italian pilots subsequently claimed eight P-47s shot down and one probable (the 325th FG lost three Thunderbolts) and three B-17s destroyed (all confirmed by Fifteenth Air Force loss records) and a fourth as a probable.

Among those credited with Thunderbolt kills was Capitano Visconti (his eighth victory), while the three B-17s fell to Sottotenente Remo Lugari, Maresciallo Gino Giannelli and Sergente Maggiore Luigi Gorrini. The 325th FG claimed ten enemy fighters destroyed, four probables and one damaged. 1° *Gruppo Caccia* lost four *Veltros* and three pilots during the action, with 1ª *Squadriglia* having Tenenti Guerrino Bortolani and Giovanbattista Boscutti killed. After successfully bailing out of his Macchi, Boscutti was fired at by a P-47 whilst hanging beneath his parachute. 3ª *Squadriglia*'s Sottotenente Bruno Castellani perished when his C.205V crashed into the sea off Venice, while squadronmate Sottotenente Andrea Stella was injured in a forced landing near Adria.

One week later, on 18 March, 1° *Gruppo Caccia* pilots were in action

A starboard side view of MM92272 6-1, and two other C.205Vs from 1ª *Squadriglia*, 1° *Gruppo Caccia*, on alert readiness at Campoformido in early 1944. Note the starter crank handles in place on two of the aircraft – key tools for the rapid despatch of Macchi fighters. It would appear that the fasces has only been applied to the uppersurface of the aircrafts' port wing *(Aeronautica Militare-Fototeca Storica)*

Sergente Maggiore Angelo Zaccaria of 2ª *Squadriglia*, 1° *Gruppo Caccia* bailed out of his C.205V on 18 March 1944 after attacking B-17s near Campoformido. Minutes later, while descending beneath his parachute, Zaccaria was machine-gunned by a P-38 and killed. The 'Angry Wasp' insignia formerly used by 3° *Stormo Caccia* was another of the *Regia Aeronautica* emblems adopted by the AR (*Aeronautica Militare-Fototeca Storica*)

again when they intercepted B-17s from the 2nd, 97th and 99th BGs between Pola and Casarsa. Thirty C.205Vs were scrambled, the fighters engaging the bombers as they approached Campoformido airfield. This time the Flying Fortresses were escorted by 90 P-38s from the 1st, 14th and 82nd FGs and around 60 P-47s from the 325th FG.

Despite being outnumbered five-to-one by USAAF fighters, *Veltro* pilots Tenente Giuseppe Robetto of 1ª *Squadriglia* and 3ª *Squadriglia*'s Sergenti Maggiori Diego Rodoz and Giampiero Svanini claimed one 'B-24' apiece. 1ª *Squadriglia*'s Sottotenente Andrea Stella and Sergente Maggiore Giuseppe Marconcini and Maresciallo Amedeo Benati of 3ª *Squadriglia* were each credited with a P-47 destroyed.

Four Flying Fortresses were in fact lost, and the 325th FG had two P-47s destroyed. The group's pilots were in turn credited with nine kills. 1° *Gruppo Caccia* lost two *Veltros* and had a third fighter damaged when it force-landed near Campoformido during a bombing raid. The first C.205V downed was the aircraft flown by Sergente Maggiore Luigi Gorrini, who took to his parachute after his fighter was hit by a P-38 from the 82nd FG. The second *Veltro* lost was flown by Sergente Maggiore Angelo Zaccaria, who, having bailed out, was machine-gunned by a P-38 and killed whilst descending beneath his parachute.

At Campoformido, two more C.205Vs were destroyed and 12 damaged by fragmentation bombs that had been dropped by the B-17s.

1° *Gruppo Caccia* was called on to intercept 20 B-24s from the 450th BG on 24 March when Campoformido was targeted once more. The bombers were attacked over the Gulf of Trieste, and two were shot down (as confirmed by USAAF records). One fell to Sergente Maggiore Diego Rodoz and the second was shared between Tenenti Giuseppe Robetto and Mario Cavatore and Sottotenente Giovanni Sajeva. A third Liberator was badly damaged by Sottotenente Franco Storchi, the aircraft being seen to drop out of formation trailing smoke and head south over the sea.

On 28 March, 1° *Gruppo Caccia* pilots celebrated Italian Air Force Day by intercepting a formation of B-24s from the 47th and 49th BWs, escorted by P-47s from the 325th FG and P-38s from the 1st, 14th and 82nd FGs. As the bombers headed for Mestre marshalling yards, they were engaged by 29 C.205Vs. In the furious combat that followed, Sergenti Maggiori Marconcini and Veronesi claimed two B-24s destroyed (not confirmed by USAAF loss records), while Tenenti Renato Talamini, Gianni Levrini, Giuseppe Rosati, Remo Lugari and Sottotenente Giovanni Sajeva each claimed a P-38 kill. Only three Lightnings were lost.

1° *Gruppo Caccia* paid a high price for these successes, losing two C.205Vs and Sergente Maggiore Alverino Capatti. His Macchi crashed near the village of Dogato, where Capatti had been born. Tragically, among the locals who rushed to the wreckage was the pilot's father, and when he realised that his son had been killed, he stood to attention and exclaimed, 'He did his duty as an Italian'.

The second aircraft lost was the C.205V of Tenente Giovanni Pittini, who bailed out after his fighter was badly shot up by a P-38. Pittini had also been wounded, his foot being so badly lacerated by an exploding cannon shell that it had to be surgically removed. Despite being an amputee, Pittini would continue to fly post-war.

The remaining 27 Macchis landed at Aviano at the conclusion of this mission, where they were refuelled and rearmed, before returning to Campoformido.

On 29 March, 155 B-24s from both the 47th and 49th BWs, escorted by 62 P-38s from the 1st and 14th FGs, attacked Bolzano marshalling yards. To counter this raid, 53 C.205Vs from all three of 1° *Gruppo Caccia's squadriglie* were led into action by Capitano Visconti. Thirty of the fighters intercepted bombers from the 98th and 451st BGs, and their Lightning escorts from the 14th FG, between Asiago and Bassano del Grappa.

Pilots claimed four Liberators destroyed – three were actually lost. A P-38 was also downed by Sergente Angelo Vezzani. These five kills took 1° *Gruppo Caccia's* tally to 50 victories in three months. Two C.205Vs were lost in return, with Sergente Maggiore Domenico Balduzzo being wounded and Sottotenente Sergio Sbrighi failing to return. He had claimed one of the B-24 victories immediately prior to his death.

April started in much the same way as March had ended for 1° *Gruppo Caccia*, with combat taking place on the 2nd when 31 C.205Vs were scrambled to intercept a largescale Fifteenth Air Force raid consisting of 548 B-17s and B-24s escorted by P-38s from the 1st, 14th and 82nd FGs and P-47s from the 325th FG. The bombers were heading north for the Steyr weapons plant in Austria.

Maresciallo Amedeo Benati claimed a B-17 destroyed over the Austrian city of Klagenfurt, this aircraft being one of eight bombers lost that day by the Fifteenth Air Force, while Tenente Giuseppe Robetto was credited with the destruction of a P-38. Three *Veltros* were in turn destroyed, with the fighters of Sergente Maggiore Aroldo Burei and Tenente Emilio Marchi colliding whilst attacking the USAAF formation. Burei bailed out wounded and Marchi was killed. Maresciallo Vittorio Pirchio also took to his parachute after he was wounded in the abdomen by a P-38, the pilot being hospitalised in Austria.

Four days later, 1° *Gruppo Caccia* fighters were sent to intercept B-17s and B-24s, escorted by P-38s from the 82nd FG and P-47s from the 325th FG, that had been sent to bomb Zagreb airfield. The Italian pilots clashed with their American counterparts over the Province of Zara and two P-47s were claimed to have been shot down. One fell to Tenente Bruno Cartosio south of Karlovac and the second was credited to Sergente Maggiore Luigi Gorrini. However, the 325th FG did not lose any fighters on this date.

The P-47 pilots in turn claimed three C.205Vs destroyed, which matched 1° *Gruppo Caccia's* trio of losses. Sottotenente Remo Lugari and Maresciallo Luigi Morosi were killed and Sergente Maggiore Gorrini was forced to bail out.

Pilots from 1° *Gruppo Caccia* undertake a pre-mission briefing on the flightline at Reggio Emilia in the spring 1944. The four aviators in the foreground are, from left to right, six-victory ace Sergente Maggiore Diego Rodoz (wearing a flying helmet), *gruppo* CO Capitano Adriano Visconti, five-victory ace Sottotenente Giovanni Sajeva and Tenente Mario Cavatore (who claimed one and one shared B-24 victories and one damaged with the AR) (*Aeronautica Militare-Fototeca Storica*)

On 7 April the USAAF targeted the city of Treviso, which was virtually destroyed with the loss of more than 1600 lives. 1° *Gruppo Caccia* scrambled 23 C.205Vs and intercepted B-24s from the 47th BW, escorted by P-38s from the 14th FG. The Italian pilots claimed three B-24s shot down, with Tenenti Antonio Weiss, Mario Cavatore and Egeo Fioroni each being credited with a victory. Two Liberators were actually lost.

1° *Gruppo Caccia* was transferred to Reggio Emilia on 24 April in order to be closer to the frontline. From here, it was hoped the unit could help counter the growing threat posed by Allied medium bombers and fighter-bombers that had commenced operations against Axis targets north of the Appennines and on the Pianura Padana. However, the C.205Vs would continue to be mainly used to oppose USAAF heavy bombers (and their escorts), which switched to hitting tactical targets in northern Italy during May.

On 25 April Capitano Visconti led 24 C.205Vs in the interception of B-24s, escorted by P-38s from the 82nd FG, heading for the Macchi plant at Varese. Lightnings were shot down by Visconti (for his ninth kill) and Sottotenente Carlo Cucchi, without loss. The outcome was not so positive four days later when Bf 109s from I./JG 77 bounced a formation of 26 C.205Vs over San Marino. In the second case of mistaken identity to befall 1° *Gruppo Caccia* since its formation, Sottotenente Luigi Bandini and Maresciallo Pietro Salvatico were killed when their *Veltros* were shot down. The German pilots involved were quick to apologise, stating that they thought the C.205Vs were Mustangs.

1° *Gruppo Caccia* was called on to defend its new home on 30 April when Fifteenth Air Force B-17s attacked Reggio Emilia with fragmentation bombs. Only modest damage was inflicted on the widely dispersed aircraft. Eighteen C.205Vs were led aloft by Capitano Visconti, and these aircraft clashed with P-38 escorts. Visconti, who was promoted to the rank of maggiore the following day, claimed a Lightning, which crashed southeast of Bologna. This aircraft would prove to be the Italian ace's fourth, and last, kill whilst flying with 1° *Gruppo Caccia,* taking his overall tally to ten.

Sergente Maggiore Domenico Laiolo achieved ace status during the course of the mission by also downing a P-38, while Capitano Pio Tomaselli claimed a third Lightning southeast of Forlì. The 14th FG recorded just one loss on 30 April, however.

Reggio Emilia was targeted again on 12 May, when P-38s from the 1st FG strafed the airfield. Eleven-victory ace Maresciallo Carlo Magnaghi was shot down during the attack, and he would succumb to his wounds the following day. Sottotenente Aurelio Morandi scrambled in the midst of the attack and managed to shoot down one of the Lightnings.

Veltro losses continued to mount during May, with Sergente Maggiore Rolando Garavaldi being shot down and killed by a P-47 from the 325th FG near Bologna on the 13th, and Tenente Bruno Cartosio's

C.205V falling to defensive fire from a 449th BG B-24 over Molinella the following day. This meant that 1° *Gruppo Caccia*'s operational strength had plummeted from 28 serviceable fighters on 10 April to just eight by 20 May. The unit struggled on with what aircraft it had, nevertheless.

On the 25th, Sergente Maggiore Luigi Gorrini claimed a B-24 destroyed over Piacenza for his 19th, and last, victory of the war – the Fifteenth Air Force lost 17 B-24s that day. Fellow ace Maresciallo Dino Forlani claimed two P-38s destroyed, but Tenente Vittorio Satta was shot down and killed by a Lightning from the 14th FG.

1° *Gruppo Caccia* was now at breaking point, both in terms of pilot numbers and serviceable aircraft. Morale was badly flagging, and to make matters worse, Sottotenente Alberto Graziani deserted to Corsica in his C.205V on 28 May. By 1 June, the unit had lost 35 *Veltros* and 28 pilots in five months of near-constant combat. In order to make good these losses, 1° *Gruppo Caccia* was issued with 50 G.55s transferred from 2° *Gruppo Caccia* and pilots from *Squadriglia Autonoma 'Montefusco'*. The Fiat fighters were issued to 1ª and 3ª *Squadriglie* and the *Veltros* (32 in total) were assigned to 2ª *Squadriglia*.

Squadriglia Autonoma 'Montefusco' was one of a handful of units that had formed spontaneously following the Armistice, being equipped primarily with G.55s, as well as a handful of C.205Vs. Commencing operations from Venaria Reale in late February, the unit was led by eight-victory ace Capitano Giovanni Bonet until his death in combat on 29 March. *Squadriglia Autonoma 'Montefusco'* was officially integrated into the defensive organisation for northern Italy on 8 April, and its pilots transferred to 1° *Gruppo Caccia* on 2 June. Having not flown *Veltros* for several months, aviators assigned to 2ª *Squadriglia* had to first familiarise themselves with the Macchi before being declared ready for combat.

On 13 June Sergente Maggiore Luigi Di Cecco was killed when his *Veltro* was shot down by a P-47 from the 325th FG northeast of Venice. Two days later, Sergente Maggiore Gorrini fell victim to a Spitfire from No 243 Sqn, and although the ace successfully bailed out of his C.205V, he was badly injured when he landed heavily. Gorrini's war was now effectively over.

Proof that Reggio Emilia was becoming increasingly untenable to operate from came on 1 July when 11 P-47s from the 57th FG bounced six C.205Vs and five G.55s shortly after they had been scrambled. The Thunderbolts had just attacked bridges in the Ferrara area and they were looking for airfields to strafe. The Macchis were providing top cover for the Fiat fighters when they were attacked, and two C.205Vs were shot down and a third forced to crash-land. Sergente Maggiore Luigi Boscaro

C.205V pilots from 1° *Gruppo Caccia* discuss a recently completed mission after landing at Reggio Emilia in early May 1944. They are, from left to right, Capitano Adriano Visconti, Tenente Mario Cavatore (who survived five emergency landings and an accident during his frontline career), five-victory ace Sottotenente Giovanni Sajeva and Tenente Vittorio Satta, who was killed in action when he was shot down by a P-38 from the 14th FG on 25 May 1944 (*Aeronautica Militare-Fototeca Storica*)

Ace Maggiore Adriano Visconti, CO of 1°
Gruppo Caccia, claimed four of his ten
victories with the AR. Having fought from
June 1940 through to April 1945, he and
his adjutant, Sottotenente Stefanini, were
murdered by partisans in Milan on 29 April
after negotiating an honourable surrender
for 1° *Gruppo Caccia* (*Aeronautica Militare-
Fototeca Storica*)

was killed, Tenente Alessandro Beretta bailed out and Sottotenente Elio
Pezzi was wounded. Two G.55 were also lost. Sergente Maggiore Mario
Veronesi claimed a P-47 destroyed in return, but no USAAF fighters were
lost (three suffered minor damage).

The following day, 1° *Gruppo Caccia* transferred 11 C.205Vs and eight
G.55s to Vicenza, with a further seven Macchi fighters making the move
on 3 July.

Shortly thereafter, morale within 1° *Gruppo Caccia* effectively collapsed.
The high casualty rate, poor fighter serviceability and constant 'interference'
by the Luftwaffe led Maggiore Visconti to put his unit's grievances directly
to the head of the recently renamed *Aeronautica Nazionale Repubblicana*
(ANR), Generale Arrigo Tessari – he had replaced Tenente Colonnello
Ernesto Botto in March after the latter was sacked for political reasons.
Dismayed by this turn of events, Tessari gave the pilots the stark choice of
either fighting on or leaving their unit and returning home. Several chose
the latter, and Visconti asked for a period of rest. Tessari's report on the
unit read as follows;

'Faith in fascism no longer animated the unit: "political doubts" masked
an unspoken weariness and intolerance of German interference. When the
real roots of the disease became clear I undertook radical surgery [15 pilots
dismissed, 21 sent on leave and seven transferred to second-line units] in
the hope of healing the unit.'

Maggiore Guglielmo Arrabito was posted in to take command of the
gruppo, and he was killed in his first mission in charge of the unit on 20
July when Mustangs of the 31st FG and Lightnings from the 14th FG
attacked ten C.205Vs and 12 G.55s that attempted to intercept B-24s over
Udine. Two Macchis and two Fiats were lost, with two pilots being killed.
A solitary Lightning was claimed as a probable in return.

Maggiore Visconti returned to lead 1° *Gruppo Caccia* on 25 July, and
that day eight C.205Vs and eight G.55s clashed with P-47s escorting
bombers over Mantua-Modena. Tenente Gian Mario Zuccarini claimed
a Thunderbolt shot down, but this action cannot be correlated with any
Allied combat reports for that day.

On the 30th, a mixed formation of 18 C.205Vs and G.55s intercepted
17 B-26s of the 17th BG near Torriglia. The medium bombers were
escorted by 12 Spitfires from No 232 Sqn, and RAF pilot WO Eddie
McCann later reported;

'Behind the Me-109, six G.55s attacked and in one head-on pass I fired
and saw strikes on the engine of one of them, followed by black smoke
as it dived away.'

All the fighters encountered by the Spitfires had in fact been C.205Vs,
and although McCann only claimed his opponent as damaged, Sergente
Maggiore Tommaso Morabito was killed when his fighter crashed near
Sampierdarena. Tenente Alessandro Beretta and another unnamed pilot
claimed a Spitfire and 'Boston' destroyed, respectively, but no Allied
aircraft were lost – Beretta's Spitfire suffered cannon shell damage to its tail.

After undertaking uneventful patrols for the first few days of August,
1° *Gruppo Caccia* was not called on again to fly. Luftwaffe personnel
drained the unit's fighters of fuel, and on 11 August 1° *Gruppo Caccia*
was ordered to move to Ponte San Pietro minus its aircraft, 24 pilots and

81 groundcrew. These would be assigned to 3° *Gruppo* at Vicenza, which also had a handful of C.202s on strength for pilot training. As it transpired, 1° *Gruppo Caccia*, which was supposed to be re-equipped with Bf 109Gs prior to moving, never received any Messerschmitts and stayed put with its mixed bag of 13 (seven serviceable) Macchis and 18 (nine serviceable) Fiats. With no fuel available, the unit was unable to undertake any sorties.

On 25 August, the Germans announced that the ANR was to be disbanded. Tired of Italian bureaucracy hindering frontline operations, *Luftflotte* 2 put Operation *Phoenix* into action. This would see the ANR replaced with an 'Italian Air Force Legion' under direct control of the Luftwaffe. All Italian airfields, and area commands, were surrounded by German troops and the following proclamation was duly read out at the various bases;

'Airmen of Italy, Soldiers of the Signals and Ground Echelons!

'Your fight is threatened with suffocation by bureaucracy and excessive administration. The Luftwaffe High Command has therefore decided, in agreement with the Italian Government, to abandon its previous methods of cooperation with the Italian Air Force.

'It is up to you to choose either voluntarily to join the newly formed Italian Air Legion, and alongside your German comrades, to fight unconditionally in the German Wehrmacht under German leadership and to fly until the common victory for the New Order in Europe and the rebirth of a new Italy, and hereby become the nucleus of an eventual great Italian Air Force, or to enlist in the Air Defence Divisions that are to be established in what has hitherto been the Italian Air Force.

'Field Marshal Freiherr von Richthofen summons you to the fight for freedom and honour and to your Homeland's defence. The fallen heroes of your people in this war are watching you. Let not their sacrifice have been in vain.

'Enlist as volunteer warriors in the new Italian Air Legion.'

The personnel of the ANR were left nonplussed by this unexpected turn of events. According to an officer who defected to the Allies in October;

'We had a choice of three courses: form part of an Italian "Air Legion" (with flying duties); enter a Flak organisation; or be transported off to a concentration camp. Those who accepted either of the first two options would have to swear an oath to Hitler, wear a German uniform and be ready to be posted to Germany.'

Despite being repeatedly threatened with deportation, the 2300 personnel of the ANR resisted the German demands to a man. Although the proclamation had stated the Luftwaffe move had the support of the Mussolini government, this was in fact a lie. When Mussolini was made aware of what was happening some three days after *Phoenix* came into effect, he immediately ordered its cessation. Nevertheless, the Luftwaffe seized 16 Bf 109s (it had no use for the ANR's few serviceable C.205Vs and G.55s) for JG 77 and forbade the fighter *gruppi* from flying.

1° *Gruppo Caccia*'s pilots would remain grounded until early November, when they were sent by train to Holzkirchen, in Germany, to begin the unit's long-delayed conversion to the Bf 109G. The *gruppo*'s switch to the Messerschmitt signalled the end for Italian-built fighters in frontline service with the ANR.

CHAPTER SEVEN

IN FOREIGN SERVICE

C.205V *Serie III* MM92247 'Yellow 17' from 6./JG 77 undertakes a training mission with a second *Veltro* from Lagnasco in November 1943. Note the aircraft's non-standard *Balkenkreuz*, which has been modified with additional black bars in order to ensure that it stands out against the white fuselage band (*Aeronautica Militare-Fototeca Storica*)

LUFTWAFFE OPERATIONS

Following the Italian Armistice in September 1943, war-weary II./JG 77 urgently required fighters to replace the heavy losses it had suffered during the summer action over Sicily. The Luftwaffe High Command decided that the most expeditious way to achieve this was to replace the *Gruppe*'s few remaining Bf 109Gs with surplus C.205Vs seized from the *Regia Aeronautica* as war-booty during Operation *Achse*, when Italian forces were disarmed by the Germans between 8 and 19 September.

Shortly thereafter, several pilots from II./JG 77 were sent to Lonate Pozzolo airfield to undertake their conversion onto the *Veltro*. Unaccustomed to the aircraft, the Luftwaffe pilots destroyed five Macchis and suffered three fatalities during an extended training period that ran from 28 September through to 24 December 1943. The first pilot to be killed was Unteroffizier Hans-Georg Soltmann on 28 September, followed one week later by six-victory ace Feldwebel Erhard Philipp of 6./JG 77.

By then II./JG 77 had 52 C.205Vs on strength, although only nine were serviceable according to a report sent by *Gruppenkommandeur* Hauptmann Siegfried Freytag to *Luftflotte* 2 HQ on 11 October. He also noted that the unit had 65 pilots, 36 of whom were ready for operations. Freytag's 4., 5. and 6. *Staffeln* were led by aces Oberleutnante Heinz Dudeck, Franz Hrdlicka and Joachim Deicke.

On 6 October II./JG 77 transferred from Lonate to Cascina Vaga airfield, and ten days later another *Veltro* was destroyed at Foligno, in central Italy, killing Gefreiter Karl-Heinz Schiller of 6./JG 77. Having suffered three fatalities in 18 days, the Germans began to suspect that acts of sabotage were to blame. However, these suspicions were dispelled by Macchi test pilot Guido Carestiato, who visited the *Gruppe* to demonstrate how the *Veltro*'s flight characteristics differed from the Bf 109G.

C.205V *Serie III* MM92247 'Yellow 17' can also be seen in this view of 6./JG 77's dispersal area at Lagnasco. The *Veltros* were only operational with the *Gruppe* from 8 November through to 31 December 1943, when they were passed on to the AR's 1° *Gruppo Caccia* (*Aeronautica Militare-Fototeca Storica*)

Declared combat-ready by the end of October, II./JG 77's *Veltros* were tasked with defending Turin. USAAF heavy bombers began focusing on industrial areas in northern Italy during November, and on the 6th of that month II./JG 77 moved to Lagnasco airfield. Two days later, the German *Veltros* went into action for the first time when they intercepted 50 B-17s. No successes were reported following this mission, however.

On 9 November, Oberleutnant Franz Hrdlicka claimed a P-38 for his 37th confirmed victory and the first of only three kills (two P-38s and a B-24) credited to German *Veltros*. His victim was either a Lightning from the 14th FG or an unarmed F-5A reconnaissance aircraft. Two days later, Unteroffizier Albert Ullrich of 6. *Staffel* claimed a B-24 south of Turin for the first of his eventual 12 victories, this being the only success he achieved in the C.205V. Finally, on 1 December, Unteroffizier Rudolf Funke, also of 6./JG 77, claimed a P-38 for his fifth, and final, confirmed kill. He was forced to bail out minutes later, however, when his fighter was hit by fire from another Lightning. Two other C.205Vs were also badly damaged in the same action, the *Veltros* having clashed with 25 P-38s over Turin. II./JG 77's Macchis subsequently failed to intercept enemy aircraft again.

On 24 December, another *Veltro* accident west of Lagnasco caused the death of Unteroffizier Schwarz. Six days later, II./JG 77 flew its final sorties with the Italian fighter, patrolling Ligurian skies between Sanremo and Varazze.

German pilots used to the heavily armed Bf 109G had found the *Veltro* poorly equipped for combat with well armoured Allied fighters and bombers. They were also highly critical of the aircraft's unreliable radio. With respect to the C.205V's flight characteristics, pilots were unimpressed by its tendency to fall into a spin when turning tightly. Finally, complicated rearming and refuelling operations hampered the swift turnaround of aircraft between missions.

II./JG 77 welcomed the return of more familiar Bf 109G-6s during the first week of January 1944, having transferred 22 C.205Vs to 1° *Gruppo Caccia* of the AR on 31 December.

CROATIAN OPERATIONS

Aside from the Italians and Germans, the Croats also flew a small number of C.202s operationally during World War 2. On 23 December 1943, interceptor squadrons were formed by the *Hrvatska Zrako Legija* (HZL – Croatian Air Legion) with the support of the Luftwaffe. At the end of January 1944, eight brand new Breda-built *Serie XII Folgores* were flown to Lučko airfield by AR pilots, followed by four more in mid-February – these fighters were part of a production batch of 60 *Serie XII* aircraft completed by Breda after the German occupation of Italy.

Eventually, 15 C.202s would arrive from Italy, although one was subsequently lost in an accident during a test flight by a Croatian pilot. The HZL had hoped to equip I./*Kroatien Jagdgruppe* 1 with Bf 109Gs, but the Luftwaffe felt it could not spare any Messerschmitts at this time.

Prior to converting onto the *Folgores* in early March, pilots destined to fly the Macchis initially received operational training on CR.42s and G.50s. Later that month, C.202 pilots on a training flight had the unit's first contact with USAAF aircraft when both fighters and bombers were spotted west of Zagreb. Combat was avoided, however, as 2./*Kro* JGr 1's pilots had quickly realised that attacking American bomber formations in lightly armed C.202s was simply out of the question. Instead, they were told to only engage damaged bombers and stragglers, as well as lone reconnaissance aircraft.

On 1 April the unit was re-designated I./*Jagdgruppe Kroatien*, with 2./JGr *Kro* operating all of the HZL's *Folgores*. Over the following three months at least four more C.202s and four C.205Vs were received. Apart from Lučko, the Macchis were flown from Zalužani, Ceravci, Pleso, Kurilovec, Sunja and Borovo airfields.

On 2 April the Fifteenth Air Force mounted a largescale raid on ball-bearing factories in Steyr. At 1100 hrs two 2./JGr *Kro* C.202s were scrambled from Lučko to intercept any stragglers on the return leg of the mission, and Eastern Front veteran narednik Bozidar Bartulovic claimed

Croat pilot cadets smile for the camera while sat on a Breda-built *Serie XII* C.202 of 2./*Jagdgruppe Kroatien* at Borovo airfield in the spring of 1944. The fighter has the underside of its engine cowling painted in RLM 04 yellow as a tactical recognition marking (*Boris Ciglic/Milan Micevski Collection*)

a B-24 destroyed. The bomber's demise could not be corroborated, so the victory remained unconfirmed.

Four days later, Zalužani airfield (near Banja Luka) was subjected to a surprise attack by Spitfire IXs of the SAAF's No 7 Wing. At least 21 Croat and 16 Luftwaffe aircraft were either destroyed or badly damaged on the ground. Among those lost were two of four C.202s that had been sent there from Lučko. The remaining pair returned home the following day.

Another fierce combat was fought with USAAF aircraft on 23 April when the Fifteenth Air Force launched a largescale raid on the Austrian city of Wiener Neustadt and the nearby towns of Bad Vöslau and Schwechat. At 1330 hrs bojnik Ivan Cenic led five C.202s in a scramble from Lučko to intercept bombers as they headed back to their airfields in Italy. Although a B-24 was shot down by vodnik Leopold Hrastovcan near Zapresic for the unit's first confirmed success with the C.202, two *Folgores* fell to Mustang escorts from the 31st FG near Bjelovar. Both pilots (one of whom was bojnik Cenic) survived after bailing out.

Some days later, vodnik Jakob Petrovic and wingman Stjeoan Klaric intercepted an RAF Mosquito west of Jastrebarsko, as the former subsequently reported;

'We spotted a recce Mosquito flying at 26,000 ft. We gained more height and were in a sound position above him when we attacked. I fired a two-second burst and hit him. He started to trail thick smoke and turned towards the sea. At that moment another Mosquito attacked us from above and we had to break off our attack. He didn't bother us much, however, diving away off towards Italy. I just managed to see the first one trailing smoke and gently losing height in the distance, but could not follow it as my fuel was getting dangerously low.'

A few weeks later, on 5 May, Petrovic again clashed with Allied aircraft;

'In early May I was flying with Ivan Kulic on a free hunt. We'd been ordered to patrol over Ljubljana–Triglev–Pula–Rijeka–Zagreb at 16,000 ft. After passing Triglev, we saw two Lightnings just beneath us, flying over the coast towards Ljubljana. We made a bit of a left turn, which positioned us up-sun. I took aim and fired at the starboard aircraft, and I could see my bullets striking its fuselage, and at that moment its stabiliser was torn off. The Lightning stalled and fell near the village of Gradiska, close to the Venice railway line. The pilot did not get out. Kulic, meanwhile, had damaged the other Lightning, but it escaped to the south.'

Petrovic and wingman vodnik Ivan Kulic had almost certainly clashed with P-38s from the 14th and 82nd FGs, which were providing withdrawal support for Fifteenth Air Force bombers that had raided Romanian targets. Both groups reported losing a single P-38 during the course of the mission, having encountered 25–30 enemy fighters (identified as Bf 109s and Fw 190s) between Nis and Kraljevo, in Yugoslavia.

In early May six pilots from I./JGr *Kro* were sent to Nis airfield to pick up four more C.202s and two C.200s, although one of the *Folgores*

A pilot from 2./*Jagdgruppe Kroatien* stands in front of a crudely 'camouflaged' C.202 at Borovo airfield in June 1944. The fighter's recently applied RLM 04 yellow fuselage band is clearly visible behind him (*Boris Ciglic Collection*)

subsequently crash-landed near Zemun airfield during the return ferry flight. The remaining three C.202s were posted to 2./JGr *Kro*, which, after several more raids on Lučko during May, sent its surviving six airworthy *Folgores* to Borovo airfield on the 29th.

Following a month of little activity from its new base, 2./JGr *Kro* was effectively wiped out on 30 June when five of the six C.202s were destroyed in an act of sabotage by pro-partisan groundcrew. This turn of events was spurred on by the state of turmoil now gripping the Croatian armed forces, with many soldiers deserting or switching their allegiance to socialist partisan groups.

Few documents concerning the operations of 2./JGr *Kro* and its C.202s survive, which is why so little is known about the unit's actions, except that its pilots were credited with four confirmed victories and between seven and 12 unconfirmed victories. Amongst the types claimed to have been shot down were two B-24s and a single B-17, Mosquito, P-38, P-51 and Spitfire. The unit's successful pilots included naredvnik Bozidar Bartulovic (unconfirmed B-24 kill), vodnik Josip Cekovic (unconfirmed B-24 kill), vodnik Leopold Hrastovcan (confirmed B-24 kill and an unconfirmed unidentified enemy aircraft), vodnik Asim Korhut (confirmed B-24 kill and an unconfirmed unidentified enemy aircraft), vodnik Ivan Kulic (confirmed P-38 kill and two unconfirmed unidentified enemy aircraft) and vodnik Jakob Petrovic (confirmed P-38 kill and an unconfirmed Mosquito).

With respect to C.202 losses, at least two were shot down in aerial combat, three were written off in accidents and five destroyed by sabotage. Only one pilot was killed, in a flying accident.

In summation, the Croat pilots and groundcrew did not rate their C.202s very high. They were hard to maintain on the ground and ineffective in the air – even against lone or damaged bombers – in skies dominated by Allied fighters. Although the Croatians appreciated the *Folgores'* superb flying characteristics, the fighters' inadequate armament meant they were ill-suited to combat against USAAF heavy bombers. The CO of 2./JGr *Kro*, bojnik Josip Helebrant, stated that the C.202s were 'old, weary and unusable', and he reported to his superiors that the morale of his pilots was 'low' and the unit's results were 'nil' as a direct result of the ineffectiveness of their aircraft.

EGYPTIAN OPERATIONS

Although Macchi was forced to halt the manufacture of C.205s following the devastating Allied bombing raids on its Varese plant in April 1944, the conversion of C.202s into C.205s continued post-war until late 1948. These aircraft were duly delivered to the *Aeronautica Militare* (AM – the new name for the Co-Belligerent *Regia Aeronautica* as of 18 June 1946), whose 5° *Stormo* retained C.202s and took over 155° *Gruppo's* C.205Vs until they were replaced by Spitfire IXs from 1947. Other examples were retained by the fighter training school at Lecce into the 1950s.

A number of the post-war C.205Vs were also delivered to the Royal Egyptian Air Force (REAF) after it ordered 80 fighters in 1947. Some 56 of these aircraft were rebuilt C.202s, with the remainder being new-build

C.205Vs. The modification programme undertaken by Macchi to turn a C.202 into a C.205 had seen the *Folgore*'s DB 601 replaced with a DB 605 and a new vertical tailfin installed. The C.202's wings were retained, however, although they now also featured underwing racks for possible stores. Lacking wing armament, the upgraded C.205Vs boasted just two fuselage mounted 12.7 mm machine guns.

A small number of the Egyptian *Veltros* would see action during the First Arab-Israeli War of 1948–49. Deliveries began on 26 September 1948, with the Macchi team sent to Egypt to oversee the fighters' introduction into frontline service being led by seven-victory ace Colonnello Ettore Foschini (formerly CO of 21° *Gruppo* on the Eastern Front). His men had crated up the aircraft prior to their shipment from Italy, and they would be responsible for their re-assembly and flight-testing once they had arrived in Egypt.

Macchi had been contracted to supply the fighters in three separate batches of 42 (11 new C.205Vs and 31 C.202s reconditioned to *Veltro* standard), 18 (three new C.205Vs and 15 reconditioned C.202s) and, finally, 20 (ten new C.205Vs and ten reconditioned C.202s). Just 15 Macchis had been delivered prior to an armistice coming into effect on 6 January 1949, bringing the First Arab-Israeli War to an end. These aircraft had arrived in four stages between 26 September and 24 November 1948. A second batch was to arrive in three stages between 17 January and 18 April 1949. A third batch never left Italy, and these aircraft were allotted to the AM for use as fighter trainers at Lecce.

The crated Macchis arrived at Almaza (near Cairo), where they would be reassembled. The aircraft had been delivered in overall medium brown *Nocciola Chiaro* (light hazelnut) paint, to which the Egyptians added dark earth. The resulting camouflage scheme left the C.205Vs looking remarkably like RAF Desert Air Force fighters from World War 2.

Painted overall medium brown *Nocciola Chiaro* (light hazelnut), this disassembled C.205V is being prepared for shipment to Egypt in 1948. It was part of the first batch of 15 *Veltros* sent by Macchi between 26 September and 24 November. All of these aircraft saw combat in the final stages of the First Arab-Israeli War (*Tony Holmes Collection*)

C.205V 1214 of No 2 Sqn in December 1948. The aircraft sports a green-outlined white fuselage band applied to REAF fighters during the latter stages of the First Arab-Israeli War. The two shades of brown used in the locally applied camouflage scheme came from old RAF paint stocks (*David Nicolle Collection*)

On 24 October 1948, C.205V 1203 was put through its paces by Macchi chief test pilot Guido Carestiato for Egyptian authorities that included Under Secretary of Air Elmeaty Bey and Fighter Units CO Col Aburabia Bey, as well as REAF squadron leaders, pilots and cadets. Comandante Carestiato's display left the assembled crowd suitably impressed. Unfortunately, one week later, C.205V 1206 was badly damaged by Colonnello Foschini in a heavy landing. The aircraft was subsequently grounded until 16 December.

Following three weeks of hard work, at least ten Macchis had been reassembled and delivered. These aircraft were then delivered to No 2 Sqn at al-Arish, in the Sinai Peninsula, where four of them became fully operational alongside the unit's Spitfire IXs. However, following the first flights by REAF pilots from al-Arish, rumours about the *Veltros'* poor performance and unreliability quickly reached Foschini. Anxious to quell the disquiet, he twice sent the Macchi team in an REAF Dakota from Almaza to visit No 2 Sqn at al-Arish. On both occasions, the transport aircraft was escorted by Comandante Carestiato in C.205V 1209.

It transpired that the alleged inadequacies had come about because of the Egyptian pilots' inexperience on type, with their uninformed views on the fighters' performance being amplified by petty rivalries among technical personnel within the squadron. As usual, impeccable flying demonstrations by Carestiato allayed any further concerns.

Meanwhile, work at Almaza continued feverishly, with Macchi engineers being urged by the REAF to speed up the delivery of fighters due to territorial gains being made by Israel on the frontline. Macchi personnel visited al-Arish twice more in December 1948, and whilst returning to Almaza on the 7th their Dakota had to be diverted to avoid Israeli fighters that were flying a sweep over the Cairo area.

Once operational with the C.205V, No 2 Sqn would undertake both interception and ground attack missions with the aircraft. The Macchis entered combat just as No. 5 Sqn, also at al-Arish, was in the process of receiving G.55s, and pilots from both this unit and No 2 Sqn flew C.205Vs into action.

Although it appears that *Veltros* may have engaged Israeli Air Force (IAF) Spitfire IXs as early as 21 October 1948, the Macchis' first official clash with the enemy came on 22 December when Israeli aircraft targeted Egyptian positions in Sinai and southern Palestine. That day, a No 2 Sqn C.205V flown by Flt Lt Shalabi al-Hinnawi was jumped with its undercarriage down on final approach to al-Arish by a No 101 Sqn Spitfire IX flown by Rudy Augarten. Despite suffering appalling wounds to his head and legs, Shalabi al-Hinnawi managed to crash-land near the runway.

On 23 December, REAF C.205Vs and Spitfire IXs participated in an attack on Tel Nof airfield, which was unopposed by IAF fighters. Another aerial battle occurred five days later when Israeli forces commenced the final offensive of the war in an effort to clear Israel of Egyptian troops in the Gaza Strip. Flying in support of the operation, Spitfire IXs from No 101 Sqn attacked the REAF airstrip at Abu Awayjila, where the C.205V flown by No 5 Sqn's Plt Off Abd al-Fatah Said was shot down by former Royal Canadian Air Force pilot Jack Doyle. During the same engagement, Gordon Levett claimed another C.205V kill. No 101 Sqn suffered damage to an S.199 fighter in return, with one being spotted trailing black smoke.

Veltro pilots flying from Bir Hama airfield claimed three IAF aircraft shot down on 29 December, but no losses were recorded by the Israelis. On the 30th, No 101 Sqn pilots Jack Doyle and John McElroy were on patrol in their Spifire IXs between Bir Hama and Abu Awayjila when they bounced and shot down two C.205Vs from No 5 Sqn. Unit CO Sqn Ldr Kamal Abd al-Wahab and Flt Lt Khalif al-Arusi were both killed. Another Macchi was shot down the following day when three Spitfires from No 101 Sqn attacked Bir Hama airfield, the aircraft being credited to Denny Wilson.

Combat continued both on the ground and in the air during the first week of the new year, with two Macchis being downed over Sinai by No 101 Sqn's Boris Senior (in a P-51D) and Seymour Feldman (in a Spitfire IX). Both REAF pilots bailed out.

The IAF claimed its final Macchi victories shortly before noon on 7 January when Boris Senior (in a P-51D) and Jack Doyle (in a Spitfire IX) escorted a Harvard dive-bomber of No 35 Flight in an attack on Deir al-Ballah airfield. The two fighters intercepted C.205Vs, and Doyle claimed one (making him an ace, as he had shot down a Bf 109 during World War 2) and Senior a probable. Four hours later, the ceasefire that had been negotiated the previous day came into effect.

As previously noted, nine more Macchis were delivered to the REAF in three stages between 17 January and 18 April 1949. The contract for supplying Egypt with its second batch of 18 *Veltros* was signed on 23 February 1949, and these aircraft were shipped in four stages between July and November of that year. With the war now over, re-assembly work by the Almaza-based Macchi team continued at a less frenetic pace, allowing Italian engineers to also undertake repairs to six combat-damaged C.205Vs.

In December 1950, a visiting technical team from Macchi noted that 26 *Veltros* remained in frontline service with units at Helwan, Almaza, al-Arish and al-Ballah. Among them were four combat veterans from 1948–49. Shortly thereafter, the C.205Vs were relegated to the role of advanced fighter trainers with the Helwan Flying School and a composite No 5/6 Advanced Combat Training School, the latter unit being based at Bilbeis in the Nile Delta. All surviving REAF *Veltros* had been grounded by the late 1950s.

REAF pilots and RAF instructor Sqn Ldr J R Baldwin (in the flight suit) pose for the camera at Deir al-Ballah in 1949. These airmen had only recently moved to this airfield after their former home at al-Arish was threatened by advancing Israeli troops. The pilot wearing sunglasses to Baldwin's left is the REAF's Chief Flying Instructor, Muhammad Hassan al-Maghribi. The remaining personnel are from No 2 Sqn. The pilot squatting to the right is Flt Lt Mustafa Shalabi al-Hinnawi, who was forced to make an emergency landing at al-Arish on 22 December 1948 after his C.205V was badly shot up by an Israeli Spitfire IX (*David Nicolle Collection*)

APPENDICES

COLOUR PLATES

1
C.202 *Serie II* MM7712 97-2 of Sottotenente Jacopo Frigerio, 97ª *Squadriglia*, 9° *Gruppo*, 4° *Stormo Caccia Terrestre*, Comiso, Sicily, 30 September 1941

Sottotenente Frigerio claimed the first victory for the C.202 in this aircraft on 30 September 1941 when he downed the 'Hurri-bomber' flown by Plt Off D W Lintern of No 185 Sqn after RAF fighters had attacked Comiso airfield. MM7712 was one of the first production aircraft completed by Macchi, the fighter then being ferried by Frigerio himself from Lonate Pozzolo to Gorizia. MM7712 was destined to have a long and varied operational life. After being fitted with a camera, it served in the reconnaissance role initially with 54° *Stormo* (being flown on occasion by ten-victory ace Capitano Adriano Visconti) and then with 377ª *Squadriglia* at Palermo (where it saw action with five-victory ace Tenente Luigi Torchio). The fighter's 'continental' camouflage scheme, nicknamed 'poached eggs' by groundcrews, featured dark green paint overall, onto which brown blotches superimposed with yellow blotches were applied. This factory finish was common to early production *Folgores* prior to the introduction of a new tropical scheme in the autumn of 1941. The 9° *Gruppo* insignia, which featured an 'iron leg' on a white triangle, is visible on the fin. It was inspired by legendary one-legged ace Maggiore Ernesto Botto, nicknamed *'Gamba di Ferro'*. Note also the all-yellow propeller spinner and nose section, which was a theatre marking used by 9° *Gruppo* on Sicily until the end of October 1941.

2
C.202 *Serie III* MM7744 73-10 of Capitano Mario Pluda, CO of 73ª *Squadriglia*, 9° *Gruppo*, 4° *Stormo* CT, Gorizia, Italy, autumn 1941

This aircraft was reportedly Capitano Pluda's mount, and it too features the 'poached eggs' camouflage scheme seen on the previous aircraft. However, the fighter lacks the yellow nose band for Sicilian operations, this marking only being applied once the aircraft was in-theatre. Aside from 9° *Gruppo*'s 'iron leg' insignia on the fin, the C.202 also has the unit's mandatory white prancing horse on a black shield on either side of its centre fuselage. Capitano Pluda, who had led 73ª *Squadriglia* since 1 March 1941 and had been credited with two victories (one shared), was killed in combat with No 126 Sqn Hurricanes over Malta on 8 November 1941 – the *gruppo* lost two C.202s and their pilots that day.

3
C.202 *Serie III* MM7726 96-6 of Sergente Maggiore Bruno Spitzl, 96ª *Squadriglia*, 9° *Gruppo*, 4° *Stormo* CT, Comiso, Sicily, 4 October 1941

As with all early series *Folgores*, MM7726 lacks both the flap marked with a red cross on the upper mid-fuselage and a radio mast. On 4 October 1941, Sergente Maggiore Bruno Spitzl force-landed this aircraft in bad weather near the Sicilian city of Syracuse. Although the fighter was badly damaged, it was recovered the following day and eventually returned to airworthiness. Spitzl went on to claim one victory and one probable in Libya in December 1941. On 11 March 1942 he was gravely injured when he crashed C.202 MM7931 on the outskirts of Milan. Spitzl passed away one month later.

4
C.202 *Serie III* MM7738 97-6 of Maresciallo Raffaello Novelli, 97ª *Squadriglia*, 9° *Gruppo*, 4° *Stormo* CT, Martuba, Libya, December 1941

MM7738 displays the white propeller spinner and nose section adopted by 9° *Gruppo* as a theatre marking for operations in North Africa. It also has standard 'poached eggs' camouflage and the dual insignia favoured by the *gruppo*. Already credited with three victories during his service in the Spanish Civil War, Maresciallo Novelli claimed a further four kills in 1941 prior to his death on 6 December. He was killed in a mid-air collision with Sergente Maggiore Anselmo Andraghetti whilst on patrol in this aircraft over Bir el Gobi in Libya. Andraghetti, in MM7745, managed to successfully bail out of his stricken *Folgore*.

5
C.202 *Serie IV* MM7409 88-7 of Maggiore Marco Larcher, CO of 6° *Gruppo*, 1° *Stormo* CT, Gabes, Tunisia, February 1943

On 31 December 1941, Maggiore Larcher officially took command of 6° *Gruppo* some two weeks after Tenente Colonnello Vezio Mezzetti had been killed in action during an engagement with Hurricane IIs from No 80 Sqn over Mechili, in Cyrenaica. By February 1943, Larcher was flying this SAI Ambrosini-built aircraft, complete with a *gruppo* CO rank pennant just below the cockpit. As with all *Folgores* completed by SAI Ambrosini, MM7409 has an extended Savoy Cross on its rudder and the white propeller spinner and nose section synonymous with North African operations. The fighter's fuselage band has been marked with the famous 'Archer' of 1° *Stormo Caccia Terrestre*, which was amongst the first units in the *Regia Aeronautica* to fly both the *Folgore* and the *Veltro*.

6
C.202 *Serie III* MM7795 90-4 of Sergente Maggiore Amleto Monterumici, 90ª *Squadriglia*, 10° *Gruppo*, 4° *Stormo* CT, Gela, Sicily, 22 May 1942

MM7795 was the personal mount of five-victory ace Sergente Maggiore Amleto Monterumici, who flew the fighter from Sicily to North Africa with 10° *Gruppo* on 22 May 1942. This *Folgore* sports the new tropical AS 'colonial' camouflage scheme of *Verde Mimetico* (dark green) mottling over *Giallo Mimetico* (sand or yellow). The *Folgore* is also fitted with a sand filter. The C.202 has 4° *Stormo*'s 4° F Baracca signature on the nose, this insignia honouring Italy's leading fighter ace of World War 1, Maggiore Francesco Baracca. This marking appeared on the cowlings of the unit's *Folgores* from 28 March 1942.

7
C.202 *Serie III* MM7806 90-1 of Capitano Ranieri Piccolomini, CO of 90ª *Squadriglia*, 10° *Gruppo*, 4° *Stormo* CT, Fuka, Egypt, summer 1942

Seven-victory ace Capitano Ranieri Piccolomini led 90ª *Squadriglia* from 20 April 1942 through to the Armistice on 8 September 1943, having also been the 10° *Gruppo* commander from 5 July 1943.

MM7806 displays the standardised AS 'colonial' camouflage scheme as seen on the aircraft in the previous profile. It also has a white spinner and the *4° F Baracca* signature on the nose cowling. 4° *Stormo*'s CO, Tenente Colonnello Armando François, ordered that the signature be applied in place of all individual *squadriglie* insignia.

8

C.202 *Serie VII* MM9113 97-10 of Capitano Fernando Malvezzi, CO of 97ª *Squadriglia*, 9° *Gruppo*, 4° *Stormo* CT, Castel Benito, Libya, January 1943

This aircraft sports the guidon-shaped rank pennant of a *squadriglia* commander beneath the cockpit, as well as the repetition of its fuselage four-number code in white on the tail cone – a rarely seen addition to the standard scheme. This particular *Folgore* was assigned to former Ju 87 pilot and ten-victory ace Capitano Fernando Malvezzi, who was CO of 97ª *Squadriglia* from 1 June to 22 October 1942 and again from 7 December 1942 through to 15 January 1943. Following the Armistice, Malvezzi joined the pro-German AR, becoming CO of 3° *Gruppo Caccia*.

9

C.202 *Serie VII* MM9083 CLIII of Maggiore Andrea Favini, CO of 153° *Gruppo*, 53° *Stormo* CT, Decimomannu, Sardinia, 12 August 1942

This *Folgore* features a number of non-standard markings. The most obvious of these are the CLIII Roman numerals on the fuselage, indicating the aircraft's status as the mount of 153° *Gruppo*'s CO, Maggiore Andrea Favini, and the blue vertical stripe that bisects the standard white fuselage band. Conversely, the *gruppo* badge, showing an *'Asso di Bastoni'* (Ace of Clubs) playing card on a blue shield, is worn in the standard position for 153° *Gruppo*. On 12 August 1942, Maggiore Favini, at the controls of this aircraft, led 14 C.202s from his *gruppo* aloft from Decimomannu airfield. They subsequently provided the fighter escort for Italian torpedo- and dive-bombers targeting the incoming 'Pedestal' convoy. The *Folgore* pilots would be credited with the destruction of five enemy fighters, and a sixth as a probable, without loss on the 12th.

10

C.202 *Serie III* MM7842 378-11 of Sergente Maggiore Faliero Gelli, 378ª *Squadriglia*, 155° *Gruppo*, 51° *Stormo* CT, Gela, Sicily, 27 July 1942

On 27 July 1942, C.202 MM7842 was one of two Macchis downed over Malta by Canadian ace Sgt George Beurling – the other aircraft, MM9042, was the mount of ace Capitano Furio Niclot Doglio. MM7842 was flown by Sergente Maggiore Faliero Gelli, who had three victories to his credit from previous engagements. The Italian pilot belly-landed his C.202 on Gozo's rocky terrain and was pulled from the cockpit in an unconscious state after smashing his face on the instrument panel when the fighter came to an abrupt halt. MM7842 features *Nocciola Chiaro* (light hazelnut) mottles over *Verde Oliva Scuro* (dark olive green), this tropical AS camouflage scheme being applied to just 30 Macchi-built aircraft between February and April 1942.

11

C.202 *Serie VII* MM9042 151-1 of Capitano Furio Niclot Doglio, CO of 151ª *Squadriglia*, 20° *Gruppo*, 51° *Stormo* CT, Gela, Sicily, 6 July 1942

A pre-war test pilot, air race winner and holder of several world speed records, Capitano Furio Niclot Doglio was also one of 51° *Stormo*'s leading aces in 1942. Over Malta, he was credited with six individual and two shared Spitfire victories in just 12 days. His mount throughout this period was MM9042, which had been ferried from Macchi to Ciampino on 16 June 1942, and then on to Gela by the 24th. The fighter sports an unusual white chevron rank pennant mid-fuselage, identifying its pilot as the *squadriglia* CO. On 6 July, Niclot Doglio badly damaged Sgt Beurling's Spitfire, only for the Canadian to take his revenge 21 days later. According to Beurling, 'The poor devil simply blew to pieces in the air' after he had fired a single burst at MM9042. Trapped in the cockpit of his disintegrating fighter, Niclot Doglio perished seconds later when the *Folgore* crashed into the sea.

12

C.202 *Serie VIII* MM8122 356-1, 356ª *Squadriglia*, 21° *Gruppo Autonomo* CT, Kantemirovka, Soviet Union, autumn 1942

A Breda-built machine, MM8122 was one of 12 *Folgores* (followed by two photo-reconnaissance C.202s) posted to 21° *Gruppo* on the Eastern Front in September 1942. The aircraft were allotted to 356ª *Squadriglia*, led by Capitano Aldo Li Greci. MM8122 displays the yellow recognition markings worn in this theatre and *Verde Oliva Scuro* mottling over *Nocciola Chiaro*. All C.202s assigned to operations in the Soviet Union were painted in this scheme, with 21° *Gruppo*'s white 'bow-armed centaur' insignia on the fin.

13

C.202 *Serie IX* MM9454 396-3 of Sergente Maggiore Gualtiero Benzi, 396ª *Squadriglia*, 154° *Gruppo Autonomo* CT, Gadurra, Rhodes, summer 1942

Macchi-built MM9454 was delivered in the standard camouflage scheme of dark olive green 'smoke rings' over light hazelnut. Being a *Serie IX* aircraft, MM9454's ventral Venturi tube was on the starboard side of the aircraft rather than beneath the fuselage – this modification was seen on all *Folgores* from *Serie IX* onwards. MM9454 also sports the *gruppo* emblem of an 'arrow-pierced hen' (with an RAF roundel on its body) just forward of the white fuselage band and the name *Mirka* on the cowling. The latter was most definitely a non-standard addition to the C.202, and was possibly the name of the pilot's girlfriend. Like most 154° *Gruppo* pilots, Sergente Maggiore Benzi fought on with the Germans following the Armistice, joining the AR when his unit was re-named the *Reparto Aereo Egeo*.

14

C.202 *Serie I* MM7913 74-2 of Tenente Giorgio Solaroli di Briona, 74ª *Squadriglia*, 23° *Gruppo*, 3° *Stormo* CT, Abu Haggag, Egypt, October 1942

A nobleman and an 11-victory ace, Tenente Giorgio Solaroli di Briona was assigned this early production *Serie I* Macchi when he was made CO of 74ª *Squadriglia*, claiming at least two of his victories with the fighter in 1942. The *Folgore* displays the usual Breda factory camouflage scheme of swirling olive green mottles over light hazelnut, with 3° *Stormo*'s 'Angry Wasp' insignia applied to the white fuselage band. In a break from the norm, the aircraft's individual red numeral has been marked onto a white triangle on its fin. This unusual feature was only seen on 74ª *Squadriglia* aircraft for a short time during the autumn of 1942.

15
C.202 *Serie X* (serial unknown) 70-5 of Capitano Claudio Solaro, CO of 70ª *Squadriglia*, 23° *Gruppo*, 3° *Stormo* CT, Medenine, Tunisia, January 1943

Although assigned to 3° *Stormo*, this aircraft lacks the unit's distinctive 'Angry Wasp' insignia mid-fuselage. Assigned to ten-victory ace Capitano Claudio Solaro, 70-5 sports 70ª *Squadriglia* numerals in white-outline form only, with the individual aircraft number being larger than the squadron number. The *squadriglia* number was also repeated on both undercarriage doors. Being a *Serie X* aircraft, the Venturi tube has been fitted to the fighter's starboard side. Capitano Solaro achieved his last victories in this C.202, with eight of them being claimed in a three-month period in 1942–43.

16
C.202 *Serie II* MM7712 377-1 of Tenente Luigi Torchio, 377ª *Squadriglia Autonoma* CT, Palermo-Boccadifalco, Sicily, February 1943

Also the subject of Profile 1, MM7712 is depicted here following its assignment to 377ª *Squadriglia Autonoma* at Palermo. The veteran aircraft was regularly flown by five-victory ace Tenente Luigi Torchio whilst with this unit, and he used it to claim a P-38 destroyed on 3 February 1943. MM7712 was damaged in the same action, however, forcing Torchio to belly land at Palermo-Boccadifalco airfield. Following the Armistice, Torchio joined the AR and was killed in combat with P-47s from the 325th FG on 30 January 1944.

17
C.205V *Serie I* MM9291 360-3 of Maresciallo Roberto Gaucci, 360ª *Squadriglia*, 155° *Gruppo*, 51° *Stormo* CT, Monserrato, Sardinia, June 1943

Ace Maresciallo Roberto Gaucci was at the controls of this aircraft when he shared in the destruction of a Marauder I from No 14 Sqn on 26 June 1943. Two days later, Tenente Mario Mazzoleni used MM9291 to participate in the downing of a P-40 from the 325th FG. This early build C.205V sports standard dark olive green 'smoke rings' over light hazelnut camouflage, with the distinctive 'black cat and green mice' insignia of 51° *Stormo Caccia* on the white fuselage band.

18
C.202 *Serie V* MM79?? '2' of Tenente Felice Figus, 374ª *Squadriglia*, 153° *Gruppo*, 53° *Stormo* CT, Palermo, Sicily, 30 June 1943

This particular *Folgore,* built by SAI Ambrosini (note the extended Savoy Cross on the rudder) was Tenente Figus' usual mount. The fighter was destroyed when Figus had to force-land it near San Michele, three miles from his airfield at Palermo, on 30 June 1943 after being shot up by two P-38s of the 14th FG. Inexplicably lacking either a unit or aircraft number on the fuselage, the fighter did, however, have the numeral '2' painted onto a black triangle on both undercarriage doors. These were added after Figus himself suggested that such numbers would be useful for pilots trying to rapidly identify their own aircraft at a distance in the event of being scrambled.

19
C.202 *Serie XIII* MM91956 368-1 of Capitano Mario Ferrero, CO of 368ª *Squadriglia*, 151° *Gruppo*, 53° *Stormo* CT, Pantelleria, Sicily, spring 1943

Capitano Ferrero led 368ª *Squadriglia* from January 1942 until he was killed in action fighting P-40s from the 79th FG over Pantelleria

on 8 June 1943. He was one of three *Folgore* pilots to die that day. Two *Veltros* were also shot down, although both pilots managed to bail out. Ferrero's C.202 was finished in typical Macchi factory-applied camouflage of dark olive green 'smoke rings' over a light hazelnut background. Being a *Serie XIII* machine, this *Folgore* had its Venturi tube fitted to the starboard side of the fuselage slightly below and ahead of the cockpit.

20
C.202 (possibly *Serie III* MM7836) 378-2 of Sergente Ferruccio Serafini, 378ª *Squadriglia*, 155° *Gruppo*, 51° *Stormo* CT, Rome-Ciampino Sud, Italy, August 1942

Seven-victory ace Sergente Ferruccio Serafini achieved all his successes flying C.202s and C.205Vs. He was killed on 22 July 1943 over Sardinia when, after shooting down a Warhawk from the 325th FG, he rammed a second P-40 with his *Veltro*, MM92156, after running out of ammunition. Eight months earlier, on 24 November 1942, Sergente Maggiore Giovanni Gambari had been at the controls of C.202 MM7836 378-2 when it was damaged by anti-aircraft fire over Tunisia. This *Folgore* has also been identified as one of Serafini's mounts during the period, and it features a 'reversed' camouflage scheme of light hazelnut blotches over dark olive green.

21
C.202 *Serie XII* MM91815 84-12 of Capitano Luigi Giannella, CO of 84ª *Squadriglia*, 10° *Gruppo*, 4° *Stormo* CT, Catania-Fontanarossa, Sicily, July 1943

Twelve-victory ace Capitano Luigi Giannella used this Breda-built C.202 to claim a Spitfire probably destroyed near Gerbini on 4 July 1943. Two days later, whilst again flying 84-12, Giannella shared in the probable destruction of a B-17 over San Salvatore with two other pilots from 84ª *Squadriglia*. On 6 August, the sabotaged remains of MM91815 were found by Allied troops when they captured Fontanarossa airfield.

22
C.205V *Serie III* MM92214 6-4 of Maggiore Carlo Maurizio Ruspoli di Poggio Suasa, 4° *Stormo* CT, Co-Belligerent *Regia Aeronautica*, Foggia, Italy, 6 October 1943

On 6 October 1943, aces Maggiore Prince Carlo Maurizio Ruspoli di Poggio Suasa (in MM92214) and Capitano Luigi Mariotti (in MM92216) flew at low-level from Foggia to German-occupied Rome, where they dropped propaganda leaflets. Ruspoli's *Veltro* was camouflaged in dark olive green 'smoke rings' over light hazelnut, this scheme even extending to the propeller spinner. The undersides were painted in standard *Grigio Azzurro Chiaro* (light blue grey), while both undercarriage doors were adorned with red/white individual and *stormo* codes. According to some sources, this unusual numeral configuration was not seen on any other aircraft assigned to 4° *Stormo*.

23
C.205V *Serie III* MM92218 'Yellow 4' of Unteroffizier Rudolf Funke, II./JG 77, Lagnasco, Italy, November 1943

II./JG 77 was the sole operational *Jagdwaffe* unit to be fully equipped with C.205Vs, and it flew them for several months before passing the fighters on to 1° *Gruppo Caccia* on 31 December 1943. MM92218 was camouflaged in the standard dark olive green 'smoke rings' on light hazelnut scheme, with light blue grey undersurfaces and a white spinner with black spirals. The latter was routinely seen on most Luftwaffe fighters of the period. Unteroffizier Funke claimed a P-38 destroyed while flying this aircraft on 1 December 1943, only to then be shot down minutes later by a second Lightning. Bailing out over Turin, he landed unharmed.

24
C.205V *Serie III* MM92212 'Yellow 1' of Capitano Marco Marinone, CO of 2ᵃ *Squadriglia*, 1° *Gruppo Caccia*, *Aeronautica Repubblicana*, Lagnasco, Italy, January 1944
This *Veltro* was the first aircraft delivered to 1° *Gruppo Caccia* by II./JG 77 to feature Italian markings, the fighter still bearing the yellow horizontal bar and individual numeral applied by its previous owner. The wing fasces painted onto the aircraft specifically to mark the C.205V's entry into service with the AR were black on a white background. The Macchi featured a standard camouflage scheme. Capitano Marinone was the first commander of 2ᵃ *Squadriglia*, and he was killed in aerial combat with P-47s of the 325th FG near Udine on 30 January 1944.

25
C.205V *Serie III* MM92277 6-2 of Sottotenente Remo Lugari, 2ᵃ *Squadriglia*, 1° *Gruppo Caccia*, *Aeronautica Repubblicana*, Campoformido, Italy, February 1944
Sottotenente Remo Lugari was credited with three victories in AR service, initially downing a P-38 with 1ᵃ *Squadriglia* on 3 January 1944. He was killed in combat with 325th FG P-47s over Croatia on 6 April 1944. Lugari's *Veltro* sports the standard 'smoke rings' camouflage scheme, with the unit's white numeral being visible on the aft fuselage and on both undercarriage doors. The fringed AR national flag, adopted on 4 January 1944 by the RSI, adorns the fuselage. Note the pilot's nickname, 'Lug', on the fuselage 'hump'.

26
C.205V *Serie III* MM92302 23-1 of Sergente Maggiore Luigi Gorrini, 1ᵃ *Squadriglia*, 1° *Gruppo Caccia*, *Aeronautica Repubblicana*, Campoformido, Italy, spring 1944
This *Veltro,* reportedly flown by 19-victory ace Sergente Maggiore Luigi Gorrini, was the last C.205V to roll off the Macchi production line during World War 2. Initially, it was delivered in the standard 'smoke rings' scheme, but this was soon replaced by Luftwaffe-inspired camouflage in three tones of grey (RLM 74/75/76). The RLM 74/75 colours were applied to the wings and tailplane, while the upper fuselage sported the lighter RLM 75 only. Note the three-colour spinner, the rear section of which was finished in RLM 75/76. The aircraft was also fitted with an RG 42 direction finding antenna on the underside of the fuselage. 1ᵃ *Squadriglia* C.205Vs were marked with red aircraft identification numbers. Having added four victories to his tally with the AR, Gorrini was shot down by a Spitfire from No 243 Sqn on 15 June 1944. Although he managed to bail out of his stricken fighter, Gorrini suffered a hard landing that badly damaged his back, forcing him into a long convalescence that brought his wartime flying to a premature end.

27
C.205V *Serie III* MM92276 15-2 of Sottotenente Aurelio Morandi, 2ᵃ *Squadriglia*, 1° *Gruppo Caccia*, *Aeronautica Repubblicana*, Reggio Emilia, Italy, June 1944
Sottotenente Morandi served with 2ᵃ *Squadriglia* of 1° *Gruppo Caccia* at Reggio Emilia, and whilst flying from here on 12 May

1944 he shot down a P-38 from the 1st FG. He followed this with a B-24 damaged on 9 June. Morandi had the unfortunate distinction of being the last 1° *Gruppo* pilot to be killed in action on 19 April 1945, being downed by Swiss anti-aircraft fire whilst chasing a B-24 in his Bf 109G. Featuring 2ᵃ *Squadriglia*'s distinctive yellow aircraft identification numbers, this *Veltro* sports the three-tone grey RLM 74/75/76 camouflage scheme and a Luftwaffe-inspired black-spiralled white spinner. The yellow-painted engine cowling was a short-lived tactical theatre recognition marking that appeared at the end of March 1944 and was then removed following an order issued to this effect by the Luftwaffe on 5 June 1944.

28
C.205V *Serie III* MM9348 of Tenente Colonnello Duilio Fanali, CO of 155° *Gruppo Autonomo* CT, Co-Belligerent *Regia Aeronautica*, Lecce-Galatina, Italy, October 1943
This *Veltro* features the Italian red/white/green roundels that replaced the fasces on aircraft serving with the Co-Belligerent *Regia Aeronautica*. Camouflaged in the 'smoke rings' over light hazelnut scheme, the fighter was adorned with Tenente Colonnello Fanali's personal insignia on the nose, which featured a winged dragon and the motto *MI FANNO UN BAFFO* ('They cannot hurt me'). The white propeller spinner had a thin red band on its tip, while both undercarriage doors were marked with large and small red arrows to denote the senior rank of the aircraft's pilot.

29
Macchi C.202 *Serie XII* 'Black 1' of bojnik Josip Helebrant, CO of 2./Jagdgruppe Kroatien, Borovo, Croatia, spring 1944
Eleven-victory ace bojnik Josip Helebrant was the commanding officer of C.202-equipped 2./*Jagdgruppe Kroatien*. 'Black 1' was a Breda-built *Serie XII* machine, being one of the aircraft delivered to the unit from *Luftpark Nis*. These Macchis featured RLM 04 yellow tactical recognition markings in the form of a fuselage band and lower cowling panel. The aircraft displayed full Luftwaffe markings over a standard Italian camouflage scheme of *Verde Mimetico* 'stains' on *Nocciola Chiaro*. The undersides were painted in *Grigio Azzurro Chiaro*.

30
C.205V 1214 of No 2 Sqn, al-Arish, Egypt, December 1948
A number of the early C.205Vs supplied to the REAF featured colours reminiscent of the RAF's Desert Air Force scheme from World War 2, these aircraft having been camouflaged in Egypt using surplus RAF paint stocks. The green-outlined white fuselage band displays the aircraft's serial, 1214, in black Arabic numerals. This fighter, based at al-Arish, suffered minor damage in late December 1948 when its pilot had to carry out an emergency landing at RAF Fayid, in the Suez Canal Zone, when he ran low on fuel.

UNIT BADGES

1
1° *Stormo*
The famous 'archer' of 1° *Stormo Caccia Terrestre* adorned some of the very first C.202s (and, later, C.205Vs) to serve with the *Regia Aeronautica*. The insignia bears the motto *INCOCCA TENDE SCAGLIA* ('Nocks-Pulls-Shoots').

2
3° *Gruppo*
3° *Gruppo Caccia*'s striking 'red Devil' badge was seen on a number of its C.202s during the summer of 1943 at Chinisia airfield, in Sicily.

3
3° *Stormo*
The 'Angry Wasp' was applied by 3° *Stormo Caccia* to its C.202s from July 1942, the insignia being seen on *Folgores* at Abu Haggag, in Egypt. The boxing gloves and dagger denoted the *Stormo*'s two sub-units, C.200-equipped 18° *Gruppo* (the gloves were inspired by its ground attack tasking) and C.202-equipped 23° *Gruppo*.

4
4° *Stormo*
4° *Stormo*'s *4° F Baracca* insignia honoured the memory of Italy's leading fighter ace of World War 1, Maggiore Francesco Baracca. It appeared on *Folgores* at Udine airfield from 28 March 1942 following an order by unit CO, Tenente Colonnello Armando François, that the signature was to replace all *squadriglie* insignia.

5
5° *Stormo*
5° *Stormo* flew C.202s with the Co-Belligerent *Regia Aeronautica* following the Armistice. There is no photographic evidence to show that the unit's 'armed Devil' insignia, complete with the motto – in Venetian dialect – *'faso tuto mi'* ('I do everything') was ever actually applied to its aircraft.

6
8° *Gruppo*
8° *Gruppo Caccia*'s medieval knight adorned the fins of the unit's C.202s during their service with the Co-Belligerent *Regia Aeronautica*.

7
9° *Gruppo*
The white 'prancing horse' of 4° *Stormo*'s 9° *Gruppo* was another insignia seen on the first C.202s to enter operational service with the *Regia Aeronautica* in July 1941.

8
10° *Gruppo*
The C.202s of 4° *Stormo*'s 10° *Gruppo* wore a black 'prancing horse' in 1941–42. Both *gruppi* badges, and especially this one in black, were inspired by Maggiore Baracca's own personnel emblem (derived from the Baracca family's coat of arms) that adorned the Italian ace's Nieuport and SPAD fighters in World War 1.

9
21° *Gruppo Autonomo*
The white 'bow-armed centaur' insignia was applied by 21° *Gruppo Autonomo* to the fins of its C.202s on the Eastern Front in 1942–43.

10
22° *Gruppo*
The famous 'spauracchio' (scarecrow) of 22° *Gruppo Caccia* was created by eight-victory ace Sottotenente Giuseppe Biron whilst the unit was flying C.200s from Tirana, in Albania, in July 1941.

According to legend, the red stars in the pipe smoke referred to the unit's successful debut on the Eastern Front on 27 August 1941, when five Soviet fighters were destroyed in aerial combat. The insignia was officially adopted by the unit shortly thereafter. This version of the 'spauracchio' was worn by the *gruppo*'s *Folgores* during the defence of Naples in 1942–43.

11
24° *Gruppo Autonomo*
24° *Gruppo Autonomo*'s armed pirate insignia was applied to a number of its C.202s during the unit's defence of Sardinia in 1943.

12
51° *Stormo*
One of the most famous insignia worn by fighter units of the *Regia Aeronautica* was the 'black cat and green mice' of 51° *Stormo Caccia*, which adorned the fuselages of its Macchis in the months prior to the Armistice. The marking was subsequently applied by the *stormo* to the fins of its C.202s during the Co-Belligerent *Regia Aeronautica* period.

13
150° *Gruppo Autonomo*
150° *Gruppo Autonomo* marked its C.202s with this insignia during the ill-fated defence of Benghazi from June to November 1942. It features the motto *GIGI TRE OSEI* ('Gigi Three Birds'), which was the nickname in the Trentino dialect of Sottotenente Luigi Caneppele, a popular *gruppo* pilot who lost his life in a flying accident in February 1942. The palms denote 150° *Gruppo Autonomo*'s North African operations, while the three stylised birds were inspired by Caneppele's glider pilot's badge.

14
151° *Gruppo*
53° *Stormo*'s 151° *Gruppo 'Asso di Spade'* ('Ace of Spades') playing card emblem looked more like a scimitar than a spade! Originally seen on the unit's C.200s, it was also applied to C.202s from early 1943.

15
153° *Gruppo*
53° *Stormo*'s 153° *Gruppo 'Asso di Bastoni'* ('Ace of Clubs') playing card insignia did indeed resemble a club.

16
1ª *Squadriglia*, 1° *Gruppo Caccia*
1ª *Squadriglia* of the AR's 1° *Gruppo Caccia* also adorned the noses of its C.205Vs with the *'Asso di Bastoni'* insignia in 1944.

17
2ª *Squadriglia*, 1° *Gruppo Caccia*
2ª *Squadriglia* of the AR's 1° *Gruppo Caccia* applied 3° *Stormo*'s 'Angry Wasp' emblem to its C.205Vs in 1944.

18
Tenente Colonnello Duilio Fanali's personal insignia
Tenente Colonnello Duilio Fanali's personal insignia recalled his prior service in the Spanish Civil War. Worn on either side of the nose of his C.205V, it featured a winged dragon and the motto *MI FANNO UN BAFFO* ('They cannot hurt me').

INDEX